How to Lead It:
Primary History

Other titles from Bloomsbury Education

How to Lead It: Primary English by Tricia Moss and Sallie Stanton
How to Lead It: Primary Maths by Shannen Doherty
How to Lead It: Primary Science by Kirsty Simkin
How to Lead It: Primary Geography by Emma Lennard
The Curriculum Compendium by Rae Snape
What Every Teacher Needs to Know by Jade Pearce

How to Lead It: Primary History

Alex Pethick
Series editor: Jon Hutchinson

BLOOMSBURY EDUCATION

LONDON   OXFORD   NEW YORK   NEW DELHI   SYDNEY

BLOOMSBURY EDUCATION
Bloomsbury Publishing Plc
50 Bedford Square, London WC1B 3DP, UK
Bloomsbury Publishing Ireland Limited
29 Earlsfort Terrace, Dublin 2, D02 AY28, Ireland

BLOOMSBURY, BLOOMSBURY EDUCATION and the Diana logo are trademarks of
Bloomsbury Publishing Plc

First published in Great Britain, 2025 by Bloomsbury Publishing Plc

This edition published in Great Britain, 2025 by Bloomsbury Publishing Plc
Text copyright © Alex Pethick, 2025

Cover design by Sophie Gordon

Typeset by Newgen Knowledge Works Pvt. Ltd., Chennai, India
Printed and bound in the UK by CPI Group (UK) Ltd., Croydon, CR0 4YY

To find out more about our authors and books visit www.bloomsbury.com
and sign up for our newsletters

For product safety related questions contact productsafety@bloomsbury.com

Contents

1 Leading history

Being a subject leader is a truly important and rewarding role. While some people step into this position because of their degree or special expertise in this subject, the truth is that many primary subject leaders find themselves taking on the role simply because there's a need for someone to do it! No matter if you're an experienced and confident leader or just starting out, this book is here to support you and help guide you along the way.

In this chapter, we will dive into the fascinating world of history. We will start by exploring important questions such as, 'What is history?' and 'Why is history important?' This is a great chance for you to think about what history means to you, and how it's being taught in your school right now. We will also consider the role of the subject leader and what this looks like in action.

In this chapter, we will:

- reflect upon the questions 'What is history?' and 'Why is history important?'
- discuss what primary history is and how we can overcome challenges we may face teaching and leading history
- look at history in the Early Years
- consider the aims of our history curriculum, looking at practical examples
- look at the role of the history subject leader.

What is history?

At first glance, you might think the question 'What is history?' is pretty straightforward. So, what do you think history is? Why not take a moment to jot down your thoughts. A quick online search might tell you that 'history is the study of the past,' but if we want to teach history effectively in our schools, we need to dig a little deeper. Understanding and appreciating the true nature of history is important, and this question is actually more complicated than it seems. In fact, it's a topic that historians often discuss and debate. Let's begin by exploring three interesting arguments that historians have presented in response to this question. Each perspective offers unique insights and adds to our understanding.

History as dialogue between past and present

One response to the question 'What is history?', put forward by E.H. Carr, is that history is a dialogue between the past and the present (Carr, 1961). Carr's famous work, *'What is history?',* rejects the notion of 'objective' historical facts and emphasises the role of the historian in carefully selecting and interpreting the facts based on their context, culture, values and perspective.

The role of the historian in creating history is central to Carr's argument. He concluded that history is a two-way stream, a continuous interaction between the past and the present, or 'unending dialogue', with each generation moulding and rewriting the past.

History as a quest for truth

In contrast to Carr, some historians have argued that history should be viewed as an empirical discipline where historians attempt to reconstruct past events as accurately as possible. Elton wrote that historians are responsible for pursuing 'objective truth' in history by uncovering and presenting facts in a way that avoids personal bias as much as possible (Elton, 1967).

History as a narrative

Another response to the question 'What is history?', put forward by historians such as Jenkins, is that history is a narrative about the past, told by the historian. Similarly to Carr, Jenkins emphasises how each generation of historians' values, cultures and perspectives shape the history they produce (Jenkins, 1991). However, while Carr compared historians with fishermen catching the fish (or facts) they want, Jenkins argues that the historian is more like a narrator who collects the information they require to create their own 'literary narrative', or story, of the past.

Your history curriculum

While primary-aged children do not need to learn about these debates among academic historians, it is helpful for us to understand the discipline's complexity. It is also worth considering what children will learn about history as a discipline through your curriculum – which we will discuss further in Chapter 3 – as well as the definitions and descriptions you provide them with to help them understand the subject better. For example, you could decide to teach children that:

- history is the stories people tell about the past.
- historians ask questions and use special ways to learn about and understand past events.
- history tells us stories that help us understand how we arrived at the present.

Why is history important?

Another question we need to ask ourselves is 'Why is history important?'

Why is history important to you? Think about it and have a go at writing down your response.

Similarly to answering the question of 'What is history?', there are many different ways of answering this. We could argue that teaching history in primary schools is important because children will study it in secondary school. However, the importance of history goes far beyond our requirement to prepare children for their next stage of education. There are so many reasons why history is such an important subject to teach. Here is a list of some of them:

1. History helps us learn from the past.
2. History helps us understand the present.
3. History teaches us how to think critically and question 'evidence' and authority.
4. History connects us to our cultural heritage and helps us understand identity.
5. History preserves our collective memory of the significant aspects of the past and develops cultural capital.
6. History enables social change and inspires innovation and progress.
7. History helps us to appreciate the complexities of humanity and society.

8. History promotes empathy and acceptance of different people, beliefs, and cultures.

9. History is needed to create informed citizens needed for democracy.

10. History is fascinating and worth studying in its own right!

While there is no right way to answer the question, these arguments can be useful in helping us reflect upon the desired impact of history in our own schools. It is worth considering these statements and reflecting upon how your history curriculum might help promote them. For example, perhaps your history curriculum includes diverse stories that reflect your school's demographic to help connect children to their cultural heritage and promote respect for different people, beliefs, and cultures. Or perhaps your curriculum teaches children about the history of democracy to help them better understand it when they are old enough to vote.

Primary history

We have discussed what history is and why it is important. Now, we are going to think about what history looks like in primary schools. In primary schools in England, children spend approximately 60 to 90 minutes learning history a fortnight (Ofsted, 2023). This means that during primary school, they will spend approximately 117 hours, or around 20 school days, focusing on history. This is not much time, so let's make each lesson count! This is why it is so vital that we carefully consider our curriculum choices. While we have to follow the National Curriculum in England, this still gives us a lot of freedom. In Chapter 4, we will look in more detail at different approaches to curriculum design.

History in the Early Years Foundation Stage (EYFS)

Children begin their introduction to history long before they experience formal history lessons. Even before starting school, children might experience stories from the past in books or television programmes. History will also be all around them from statues in the park to war memorials, old buildings and museums.

In Early Years settings in England, seven areas of learning and development need to be taught and one of these areas is 'Understanding the world.' By the end of the EYFS, the Early Learning Goals (ELGs) for 'Understanding the world' include 'Past and Present'. This means that children at the expected level of development at the end of the EYFS will:

- talk about the lives of the people around them and their roles in society.
- know some similarities and differences between things in the past and now, drawing on their experiences and what has been read in class.
- understand the past through settings, characters and events encountered in books read in class and storytelling (DfE, 2023).

The ELGs are an assessment point for the end of the reception year; they are not a curriculum. It is up to schools to design their own curriculum to ensure that all children can meet the ELGs. Therefore, if you have Early Years classes in your school, it is important that you understand what they are teaching and why. Even though their formal history education does not start until Key Stage 1, children should be exposed to some history to ensure they can meet the 'Past and Present' ELG. As a subject leader, consider how choices in EYFS support with building understanding over time. For example, perhaps they read stories about kings and queens in the EYFS in preparation for learning about British monarchs in Key Stage 1 and Key Stage 2.

Teaching history in the EYFS will differ from teaching history in Key Stage 1 and Key Stage 2. Historical understanding could be developed by singing songs, reading stories, taking trips into the local community and through play. Our Early Years classrooms have the incredible opportunity to spark a lifelong passion for history that can flourish throughout a child's life.

Overcoming challenges for primary history

While history is a fascinating and popular subject, you may face several challenges teaching it in your school. One challenge many schools find is that it can be hard to find enough time to meet the expectations set out in the National Curriculum in England. There is so much for us to do in schools that history competes with all the other subject areas. As it is not externally assessed, it is sometimes considered less important than subjects like English, maths and science. If that is the case in your school, part of your role as a subject leader is to be the voice for history. You may want to consider how you could raise the profile of the subject to ensure that it is taught well. For example, you could decide to lead a staff meeting, or support teachers with timetabling history and deciding what to teach. Another way you could put a spotlight on history is to explore opportunities for enrichment, such as school trips or inviting speakers in.

Another challenge you may face is that sometimes history is taught within a broader topic, which means that children struggle to identify between subjects, and history lessons contain activities that do not build historical understanding. For example, children might build Tudor houses out of cardboard or perform a dance as part of a topic. Chapter 4 will discuss the pros and cons of teaching history as part of a topic compared with teaching it discretely. If this is happening in your school, consider making sure children are aware they are studying history when the lesson is history-focused so that they can begin to build an understanding of the discipline.

Making sure our history lessons are relevant and accessible for young children is another challenge. It is important to consider our children's age and level of chronological understanding when teaching history. Young children tend to live in the present and find the concept of the past hard to understand. They also struggle to grasp the mathematical knowledge needed to use timelines and understand the scale of time passing. Therefore, in the first few years of their history education, you must remember that children are in the early stages of developing their chronological understanding and will require a lot of support. You may support their learning by ensuring your curriculum is relevant to them, teaching them about more recent events or history in their local area. This does not mean we cannot teach younger children about the more distant past, but we must understand that the children will be unable to comprehend how long ago this took place. Even as adults, we find it challenging to fathom the scale of time passing properly; I was shocked to discover that Cleopatra lived closer to the invention of the smartphone than the construction of the Great Pyramids! In Chapter 6, we will look at ways to support children with this.

Another consideration when teaching history is children's level of maturity in primary school. Children differ significantly from adults in terms of their knowledge of the world and understanding of human behaviour and relationships. Therefore, when you teach history, you must remember that children do not share the same knowledge as adults and some areas of history can be scary and inappropriate to discuss with young children. Consequently, you should carefully consider what you are teaching children and use explicit teaching and modelling to provide all children with the knowledge they need to access and understand your history curriculum. We will discuss this in more detail in Chapter 5.

Aims of history in your primary school

As a history subject leader, part of your role may be setting out your subject's aims or vision. To do this, you first need to consider the two important questions we discussed at the beginning of this chapter:

- What is history?
- Why is history important?

You might also want to consider the aims or vision of your whole school. What is important to your school community? Do you have school values or a school motto? How does your subject promote and enact the aims or values of your school?

Some schools create curriculum documents that set out the aims or vision for each subject. These need not be lengthy documents but should capture your intention for your curriculum and why. You do not have to write these down in a document, but you need to be clear about your aims for history in your school. If you decide against creating a document, you may reflect upon this and share and discuss your thoughts as a school instead. Alternatively, you could keep the aims short and sweet, such as:

'The History curriculum at X has been designed to be diverse, knowledge-rich, and coherently sequenced to enable pupils to develop a deep understanding and appreciation of the discipline of history.'

Whatever you choose to do, it is important that you have clear intentions for history in your school and can explain how you plan to deliver on these aims. It is also worth noting that part of your role is to communicate these intentions with teachers so that this vision is known, understood, and shared by all.

Case study A: promoting school values within the history curriculum

Stuart is a subject leader at a small rural primary school. The senior leadership team has asked him to create a document outlining the school's aims for history. After reading this chapter, he reads through his school's aims and considers how they are enacted through the history curriculum. For example, one of his school aims is to 'create passionate future citizens who are committed to creating positive change.' He considers how their history curriculum can support pupils with this by teaching children about different societies in the past and about how change happens over time, for example, when they learn about the suffrage movement. He concludes that one of the main aims of their history curriculum could be to 'enable social change and inspire innovation and progress.'

Case Study B: promoting school values within the history curriculum

Laila has recently taken on the role of history subject leader at a large inner-city primary school. Like Stuart, she has been asked to write a document explaining their history curriculum's aims. Laila wants their history lessons to reflect the diverse demographic of their school to ensure all children see themselves through the curriculum. Her school's values include respecting and valuing the diverse perspectives and identities of all individuals within their school community. Therefore, Laila writes in her document that one of the core aims of their history curriculum is to promote empathy and acceptance of different people, beliefs, and cultures.

The role of a primary history leader

Your main role as a history subject leader is to ensure that high-quality teaching and learning take place in history at your school. Wherever you are on your journey in your school, your aim should be to raise standards and plan for improvement. Here are some aspects of your role, broken down.

1. Curriculum development

Developing your school's history curriculum will involve:

- developing and regularly reviewing the subject's vision, aims, and purpose
- overseeing curriculum planning to ensure the curriculum is rich, ambitious and well-sequenced
- ensuring consistent curriculum implementation, including adequate timetable allocation
- implementing effective assessment systems to monitor pupil progress and curriculum impact
- ensuring an inclusive curriculum that supports all pupils, including children with SEND and EAL
- taking overall responsibility for pupil achievement and standards in history
- keeping up to date on relevant research and best practice related to history teaching.

2. Resourcing

Resourcing history provision in your school will involve:

- managing the subject budget effectively, spending in ways that add value and enhance learning
- pursuing additional funding from external sources when needed
- supporting literacy departments with history books and materials
- auditing and updating resources to align with curriculum and children's needs.

3. Reviewing and developing teaching and learning

Reviewing and reflecting on the quality of teaching and learning in your school and plan for improvement can be done in several ways:

- data analysis
- learning walks
- moderating assessment
- observing lessons
- checking planning and resources
- pupil voice (using informal interviews with small groups of children, talking to the school council, or using children's questionnaires)
- book looks (reviewing a small sample of children's books from each class).

4. Supporting colleagues

You can foster a supportive working environment by:

- leading a cohesive team and regularly updating on subject developments
- guiding staff on teaching, learning, resources, and planning
- offering feedback and PD based on classroom observations
- assisting with assessments.

5. Raising the profile of history and enrichment

Promoting engagement with history could include:

- running history clubs
- organising history trips
- promoting history competitions and history quality marks
- hosting history events and visits, e.g. history workshops or inviting local historians to speak
- considering how to involve and keep parents and carers informed, e.g. through the school website, newsletters, interactive homework and projects or family learning nights.

Looking at this list can seem daunting. However, it is important to remember that Rome was not built in a day! As a subject leader, you will likely be asked to write an action plan to set key areas of improvement. This list can support you in considering what you want to prioritise and when. The key is to remember that change takes time, and your school will have other areas to prioritise too, so plan for small steps and consider how you will raise standards over the next year and beyond. As you work your way through this book, we will look at some of these areas in more detail and at the end we will consider how we can implement change through our action plans.

How this book can support you

Throughout this book, we will delve into different aspects of primary history to provide you with a strong foundation from which to teach and lead the subject. You will find:

- examples of best practice from across key stages
- case studies for further exemplification
- suggestions for staff professional development
- reflection questions to help you structure your thoughts and identify next steps
- follow-up reading and resources if you want to explore a particular area further.

In the next chapter, we draw insights from the latest research together with evidence related to the practice of history teaching. We then look at how you can take an evidence-based approach yourself.

We next look at curriculum design in history. This involves exploring substantive and disciplinary knowledge (Chapter 3) and the key principles of curriculum design (Chapter 4).

You will then find detailed chapters on specific areas of the subject: historical enquiry (Chapter 5), narratives and storytelling (Chapter 6), disciplinary literacy (Chapter 7) and progression and assessment (Chapter 8). We finish with guidance on implementing improvement and change (Chapter 9).

Chapter summary

- As a subject leader, it is helpful to consider 'What is history and why is it important to me and my school?'
- Subject leaders need to be aware of what children learn in EYFS, as well as Key Stage 1 and Key Stage 2.
- As subject leaders, we must be clear about our school's aims for history. We may wish to articulate these in a document.

Questions for reflection

- What is history?
- Why is history important to me and my school?
- What are the aims of history in our school?
- How does the history curriculum support the broader aims of our school?

Example PD session: enacting school values through the history curriculum

Here is an example of what a PD session on enacting school values through the history curriculum could look like.

TIMING SUGGESTION	SESSION GUIDANCE
2 mins	Revisit your school's aims. These might be referred to as your vision or values statements. Reflect upon why these are important to you and your school.
5 mins	Share with teachers a few examples of how your school values can be enacted through the history curriculum.
15 mins	Present teachers with a list of statements about why history is important and ask them to order and discuss them. You may wish to use the ones provided in this chapter or write your own. Decide which ones are most important for your school.

TIMING SUGGESTION	SESSION GUIDANCE
10 mins	As a school, agree on your core aims for history teaching. These can be written up and shared with the school community.

Explore further

- *What Is History?* (1961) by E.H. Carr
- *Re-thinking History* (1991) by K. Jenkins

2 Getting the best from research evidence

As a history subject leader, your main priority is ensuring that high-quality teaching and learning take place in history at your school. To do this well, you need to make sure that your decisions to improve teaching and learning are evidence-informed. This chapter will help guide you in reviewing research and reflecting on how to effectively apply evidence in your school. In this chapter, we will:

- consider some guiding principles when engaging with research and evidence.
- summarise useful evidence bases we can use.
- look at how key insights from cognitive science can help us understand the process of learning and, importantly, how these can be applied to teaching history.
- provide examples of what this looks like in practice.

Guiding principles

When making evidence-informed decisions, you will need to draw on both external evidence, such as research, and internal data from your own context, such as what has and has not worked in the past. The decisions we make about what to implement in our schools come with an 'opportunity cost'. This means that the more time that is devoted to less effective strategies, the less time there is to spend on more effective ones. Therefore, you need to invest time to select the right solution. These three strategies can be useful in guiding decisions:

- **Prioritise large scale studies:** Where possible, focus on research with substantial sample sizes. Leaders are not interested in how an intervention worked for the pupils within a study; instead, they're interested in whether the same intervention might be beneficial for their pupils. Bigger samples tend to allow for more generalizable conclusions.

- **Maintain a critical perspective:** A large sample size doesn't automatically guarantee high-quality research. Examine the participant selection process and attrition rates. The age of the participants is also important. Much research is conducted on secondary students (or even undergraduates). Therefore, we must be cautious of applying findings about older pupils to those in primary without careful consideration. Equally, longitudinal studies based on primary pupils can have large attrition rates as pupils move to other schools, new pupils join, new teachers join the project, and so on. If subject leaders plan to base decisions on a study, they should scrutinise it thoroughly.

- **Steer clear of educational fallacies:** The field of education is rife with myths, misconceptions, and outdated ideas that persist despite being disproven (de Bruyckere et al., 2015). While you can't be aware of all of these, familiarising yourself with the most common or harmful ones can save time and help focus on more promising approaches. For example, harming myths that still exist include: people have different learning styles and you learn better if you discover things for yourself. A report released by the Sutton Trust titled, 'What makes great teaching?' includes a useful section on 'ineffective practices', which is a good starting point for subject leaders (Coe et al., 2014).

Useful evidence bases

As a busy history leader, it can be challenging to find the time to read and digest all the research available to help you make important decisions in your school. Thankfully, there are some organisations available to support you by providing up-to-date access to some of the most important findings from research in an accessible format for schools to use.

The Education Endowment Foundation (EEF)

The EEF is an independent charity that was set up in 2011 to improve the educational attainment of the poorest pupils in England. The Foundation helps schools, colleges and Early Years settings improve outcomes through the better use of evidence. This may be through their guidance reports that review the evidence base for a range of strategies developed to support specific areas, or it may be through conducting research into the efficacy of specific strategies. While they do not currently offer guides specifically for history, their 'Teaching and Learning Toolkit' is a useful starting point when considering how to support teachers to improve their practice.

The Chartered College of Teaching

The Chartered College of Teaching is the professional body for teachers. Membership gives access to research, resources and the journal *Impact*. The College produces evidence summaries that collate and review research into short digests and the journal has regular contributions from practitioners as well as researchers.

Historical Association

The Historical Association is a UK charity for history. It provides resources and support for primary and secondary teachers and subject leaders, including resources, events, professional development and its magazines *Primary History* and *Teaching History*. It is important to remember that many of the articles published in the magazines are opinion pieces written by practitioners in one context.

Blogs, podcasts and useful websites

In addition to these useful organisations, social media platforms can also offer a helpful starting point to engage with researchers and other teachers and leaders. Podcasts are useful to listen to 'on the go' and blogs can provide useful sources of practical advice. There are also a number of websites that can be useful for history subject leaders. Here are some examples of podcasts, blogs and websites that you might want to engage with.

PODCASTS	
Thinking Deeply About Primary Education https://www.youtube.com/@TDaPE	Researchers and teachers discuss teaching, learning, pedagogy, knowledge, curriculum and all things education.
Teacher Talk Radio https://www.ttradio.org/history	A live online community radio station for teachers and leaders. They have a history collection and host events specifically on teaching history.

PODCASTS

The Evidence Based Education Podcast https://evidencebased. education/podcast-archive/	The podcast discusses key issues in the field of evidence-based education, particularly focusing on how gaps between policy, research and practice can be bridged.
Mind the Gap https://www.youtube.com/c/ mindthegapwithtomemma	The hosts interview experts from the US, UK and beyond to share timely insights on YR – Y13 trends, research-based approaches in need of greater reach and strategies to close global gaps.

BLOGS

Clio et cetera
Michael Fordham
http://clioetcetera.com

The Dignity of the Thing (no longer updated)
Christine Counsell
http://thedignityofthethingblog.wordpress.com

Primarytimerydotcom
Clare Sealey
http://primarytimery.com

Mr T Does History
Stuart Tiffany
http://www.mrtdoeshistory.com

The Primary Knowledge Curriculum
Insights
http://primaryknowledgecurriculum.org/insights/

WEBSITES

Meno Academy
http://www.meno.academy

BBC Bitesize
KS1 and KS2 History
http://www.bbc.co.uk/bitesize

On This Day in History
http://www.onthisday.com

Considering context

It is always important to consider your unique school context when implementing new ideas. Even when research shows something works well, leaders must consider whether it is right for their school. What worked before doesn't guarantee future success (Major and Higgins, 2019). Your school might have special challenges that could make a new idea harder to use and you might need to do some preparation work to help a new idea succeed. It's also important to think about how much time and money a new plan will take. Before trying anything new, subject leaders should always think about their own school. You need to consider if it's possible for you to implement this, if you can afford it, and if you have the time and capacity to make the change a success. This careful thinking helps ensure new ideas have the best chance of working well in your school. We will explore how to successfully implement ideas from research in Chapter 9.

What does the research say about cognitive science?

As a subject leader, it is important to understand how children learn. For many years, teachers have relied upon intuition about learning and the best strategies to use. Thankfully, the field of cognitive science can now offer research evidence into how our brains work. Principles of cognitive science are usually derived from two key areas of research – cognitive psychology and cognitive neuroscience. Insights from these areas can help us understand more about learning, memory and the brain, which can be used to help inform our teaching and learning strategies. We now have access to many books and resources that can support us in applying findings from cognitive science to the classroom. Some of these are listed below under 'Explore further'. However, it is worth noting that the evidence for the successful application of cognitive science in the classroom still requires further research.

A good starting point for understanding one of the key insights from cognitive science is looking at the theoretical model of working memory (Baddeley and Hitch, 1974) that has been explained by Willingham (2009). Here is a concise overview:

- **Working memory:** this acts as our brain's processing centre, briefly holding small amounts of new information. On average, a person can hold about four chunks of new information in their working memory (Cowan, 2010). Though it has been found that this may be even lower in primary-aged children (Gathercole and Alloway, 2004).

- **Learning:** this occurs when we successfully move new information from working memory into long-term memory.

- **Cognitive overload:** learning can be hindered or halted if working memory becomes overwhelmed, such as when we're faced with processing too much new information simultaneously.

- **Optimising load:** learning is enhanced when instructional decisions are made to reduce extraneous load (load unrelated to key learning).

- **Cognitive overload:** learning can be hindered or halted if working memory becomes overwhelmed, such as when we're faced with processing too much new information simultaneously.

- **Long-term memory:** our long-term memory organises and stores information in structures called 'schemas'. These schemas can range from simple, containing just a few pieces of information, to highly complex, encompassing vast amounts of data. The capacity of long-term memory may be finite.

It is also helpful to be aware of research on retrieval practice (such as Pashler et al., 2007 and Agarwal et al., 2021):

- Frequent recall of learned material can enhance pupils' retention. The act of retrieving information reinforces the information in memory and reduces the likelihood of forgetting.

- Retrieval is most effective when pupils have started to forget the material, as this requires more mental effort during recall, thereby strengthening memory connections. For optimal results, retrieval practice should be spread out over time rather than concentrated in a single session.

We will discuss the use of retrieval practice in history in more detail in Chapter 5. Research in cognitive science helps us to understand how learning occurs and has several implications for the classroom:

- **Targeted planning:** Pupils need to concentrate on essential knowledge, skills, and concepts. Teachers should design activities that direct pupils' focus to these core elements. For example, if you want the children to learn about Stonehenge, rather than asking children to design their own prehistoric monument, focus the lesson on drawing, labelling and describing Stonehenge using the vocabulary you have explicitly taught.

- **Build on existing knowledge:** Pupils understand new ideas by relating them to what they already know. Teachers should begin their planning by assessing and building upon pupils' prior knowledge. For example, if you are teaching a unit on early Islamic civilisation and Baghdad in 900 CE, you could start the lesson by retrieving what pupils already know about Islam from their RE lessons.

- **Manage cognitive demands:** Pupils' working memory can easily become overwhelmed with new information. Teachers should be mindful of the cognitive load they impose and plan to introduce new material in manageable segments. For example, rather than introducing a long list of defined new vocabulary at the start of the lesson, teachers could focus on a few core words and definitions first, and then introduce other key words in context as they arise during the lesson.

- **Foster fluency:** To develop deep understanding and fluency, pupils need to revisit and apply important content regularly. Teachers should plan for frequent review, retrieval practice, and ample opportunities for pupils to apply what they've learned. For example, you may identify core concepts that children will encounter across the curriculum, such as 'monarchy', 'democracy' and 'empire'. It is important that children revisit and apply these concepts in different contexts to build a deep understanding of their meaning.

- **Adjust support levels:** As pupils develop a more sophisticated understanding of a subject area, they require less teacher guidance and scaffolding. Teachers should continuously assess pupils' understanding and adjust their level of support accordingly, matching it to pupils' growing expertise. For example, rather than always providing a scaffold, such as a writing frame for an extended write or a sentence stem, teachers should use assessment to consider whether this scaffold is still needed or whether the child would benefit from having less guidance. It is worth remembering that scaffolding on a building is removed once it is safe to do so – we can adopt the same principle in our classrooms.

Case study: applying research to practice

Emily is a subject leader at a two-form-entry primary school in the North of England. After conducting a learning walk, book look and pupil voice, she notices that pupils spend a lot of time doing 'research' in history lessons. Teachers expect pupils to discover the core knowledge themselves, rather than explicitly teaching them, as they believe this is a more effective way to learn. After reading *How Learning Happens,* by Kirschner and Hendrick, Emily understands that research from cognitive science suggests that children should not be treated as mini experts expected to solve their own problems through independent research, and that they learn better through explicit teaching, rather than discovery learning (Kirschner and Hendrick, 2020). Therefore, Emily concludes that the school could benefit from training on research-informed practice and speaks with her senior leadership team to consider how to introduce this. Following discussions, it is agreed that they could benefit from speaking with a local school that has been focusing on research-informed practice, including the use of Rosenshine's 'Principles of Instruction', explicit instruction and retrieval practice. After arranging a visit to the school to learn more about what they are doing and why, Emily's SLT enlist the support from the leadership team at the local school to work with Emily to plan for professional development and support for teachers.

Chapter summary

- Subject leaders should base their decisions on robust and reliable educational research, considering both external evidence and information from their own context.

- Guiding principles for research evaluation: focus on large-scale studies, maintain a critical perspective when examining research, and be aware of common educational myths and misconceptions.

- Learning is a cognitive process and key insights from cognitive science help us to understand the learning process and, more importantly, how these can be applied to teaching history.

- Having a secure grasp of key cognitive science is important for subject leads and should guide decisions that are made.

Questions for reflection

- How do I currently use research when deciding to implement new strategies in our school?

- In what ways am I currently considering the specific context of our school when implementing new teaching strategies?

- How well do I and teachers at my school understand and apply principles of cognitive science, such as working memory limitations and retrieval practice, in our history lessons?

Example PD session: working memory

Here is an example of what a PD session on working memory in history could look like.

TIMING SUGGESTION	SESSION GUIDANCE
10 mins	Introduce the simple model of memory from Willingham and explain the role of the working memory and the long-term memory.
15 mins	Explain to teachers that the working memory is limited and demonstrate how 'chunking' information based on knowledge in our long-term memory can help us remember more. You can provide an example, such as asking teachers to try and remember this: 110169713648 Then show them this: 106618371914 Explain that people tend to find it easier to remember the second one as the numbers can be chunked into memorable dates (1066 – the Battle of Hastings; 1837 – Queen Victoria's reign begins; 1914 – the start of World War I). If you have this background knowledge, it is easier to remember these numbers.

TIMING SUGGESTION	SESSION GUIDANCE
15 mins	Explain that we can assist our pupils in leveraging their background knowledge to support with new learning by activating prior knowledge at the start of the lesson and helping children make connections. Provide some examples, such as: • Use a timeline with time periods and events previously studied to make connections between new learning and what they already know. • Use a quiz to retrieve prior knowledge and then explain how this knowledge connects with what they are learning now.
10 mins	Ask teachers to review their next history lessons and give them time to consider how they will help children activate their prior knowledge to learn new content.

Explore further

- Rosenshine's 'Principles of Instruction' (2012), found in *American Educator* volume 36

- 'Why Don't Students Like School?' by Daniel Willingham (2009), found in *American Educator* volume 33

- *What Every Teacher Needs to Know about Psychology* (2016) by David Didau and Nick Rose

- *Understanding How We Learn* (2018) by Yana Weinstein and Megan Sumeracki with Oliver Caviglioli

- *How Learning Happens* (2024) by Paul Kirschner and Carl Hendrick

- The Learning Scientists Podcast

- The Inner Drive training and resources online – www.innerdrive.co.uk

- *The ResearchED Guide to Explicit and Direct Instruction* (2019) edited by Adam Boxer

3 Substantive and disciplinary knowledge in history

In this chapter, we will discuss the two main types of knowledge in history:

- **substantive knowledge:** knowledge of *the past*
- **disciplinary knowledge:** knowledge of *the discipline*

Appreciating the distinction between substantive and disciplinary knowledge is really useful for both curriculum design and practice. Therefore, it is key to understand what they mean. This chapter will break down these terms and show you how you can apply them in primary history. In Chapters 4 and 5, we will build on this knowledge by looking at how to use these terms when designing your curriculum and teaching history.

In this chapter, we will:

- discuss the importance of substantive and disciplinary knowledge.
- identify what 'substantive concepts' are and how they are useful in supporting pupils with understanding new content.
- unpick disciplinary concepts in history and discuss how we can teach them in a purposeful way in primary school.
- provide example questions that can be used in Key Stages 1 and 2.

Substantive knowledge

Substantive knowledge in history refers to *knowledge of the past*, sometimes called 'historical content'. From ancient Sumer to the twentieth-century space race, substantive knowledge is a term we use to describe all the historical content we teach across the curriculum. Substantive knowledge is important as we use what we know to interpret, understand and question what we hear, see, and read. Substantive knowledge also helps pupils develop chronological understanding. A well-planned curriculum allows pupils to learn about different times and places, organising this knowledge into their, 'mental timeline' (Ofsted, 2021). Therefore – as we will discuss in Chapter 4 – when designing your curriculum, you should carefully select the content you teach to build substantive knowledge over time. One way you can do this is to ask yourself three important questions:

1.   What specific knowledge of the topic do the pupils need? (e.g. knowledge of the Roman empire, Roman armies and significant people such as Julius Caesar or Boudicca).

2.   What knowledge of the historical period is needed? (e.g. broader knowledge of ancient civilisations).

3.   Is there any wider historical knowledge needed that could further support understanding? (e.g. an understanding of the concept of empire).

Substantive concepts

The language of history is often highly abstract (Chapman, 2017). Historians use a variety of abstract and general nouns and verbs to convey important concepts, such as 'democracy', 'invasion', 'colonisation', and 'monarchy'. These concepts, known as 'substantive concepts', are concerned with the substantive content of the history being studied. Unlike disciplinary concepts (which we will discuss later in this chapter), substantive concepts are harder to specify as there are many more of them, and their use and meaning are intrinsically linked to the history being studied. Cooke categorised some of these concepts as follows:

- **roles:** leader, pharaoh, monarch, minister, emperor, servant
- **structures:** government, monarchy, republic, empire
- **processes**: invasion, conquest, colonisation, reform
- **actions:** rule, migrate, deport, pass (a law) (Cooke, 2009).

Lee argues that having access to a range of substantive concepts enables pupils to transform factual knowledge into usable knowledge (Lee, 2011). Many of these concepts, such as 'monarchy' and 'democracy', feature in many contexts across the history curriculum and are important in helping pupils understand new material. Other concepts are more specific to the period, person, or event being studied (such as the Enlightenment). It is also worth noting that some of these broader concepts may encompass more specific ones, e.g. religion is a broader concept which encompasses Christianity which encompasses Calvinism.

You should plan to teach substantive concepts in meaningful contexts, enabling repeated encounters with some concepts to support pupils' understanding of new content. For example, children may first come across the concept of 'monarchy' when they are taught about significant individuals such as Elizabeth I or Queen Victoria in Key Stage 1, and then again in Key Stage 2 when they learn about the Shang Dynasty and Anglo-Saxon Britain, and then finally when they study the changing power of monarchs as a theme in British history.

All concepts must be historicised and discussed in context. While working definitions are useful, it is important that pupils recognise that these concepts can have different meanings in different contexts. Therefore, memorising fixed definitions can be problematic. For example, 'monarchy' in the thirteenth century looked very different from 'monarchy' in the seventeenth century, and the reign of Charles I certainly looked very different from the reign of Charles III today!

Here is a list of some substantive concepts you might wish to include in your curriculum:

KEY STAGE	CONCEPTS	
KS1	monarchy	invasion
	law	protest
	religion	democracy
KS2	monarchy	invasion
	law	protest
	religion	democracy
	society	settlement
	migration	dynasty
	trade	alliance
	rebellion	industrialisation
	hierarchy	empire
	parliament	church

Disciplinary knowledge

Disciplinary knowledge relates to *knowledge of the discipline*. In history, this means knowledge of how historians investigate the past, make meaning, and construct historical claims, arguments, and accounts (Ofsted, 2021). While the disciplinary dimension is less relevant in some primary subjects, (such as in languages) in history, pupils need to encounter 'rich disciplinary knowledge to refine pupils' appreciation and practice of historical argument' (Foster, 2013 and Counsell, 2018a). While secondary history teachers have a strong tradition of placing emphasis on the disciplinary aspect of pupils' learning (Ofsted, 2021), we do not need to wait until Year 7 to introduce this to our pupils. In fact, the National Curriculum in England states that from Key Stage 1, children should be taught to understand some of the ways in which historians find out about the past (DfE, 2013).

Counsell describes disciplinary knowledge as the part of the subject where pupils understand each discipline as a 'tradition of enquiry with its own distinctive pursuit of truth' (Counsell, 2018a). The idea of 'truth' in history differs from our everyday understanding. From a young age, our pupils will have been encouraged to 'tell the truth'. This can lead them to believe that there is one fixed 'truth' and anything other than the 'truth' can be thought of as a lie. However, in history, there is not one true account of the past. This does not mean that differing accounts of the past are false or that historians are not concerned with truth. Lee argues that history should be considered an 'organized metacognitive tradition' as historians must 'reflect on what they say, justify their arguments, and explain their thinking' (Lee, 2011, p.66). In our primary classrooms, you can begin to build the foundations for understanding this by explaining that in order to be taken seriously, historians need to provide enough evidence to support their claims. When answering questions in history (as we will discuss in Chapter 5) you should allow time for discussing claims, justifying arguments and explaining thinking. Over time, we want our pupils to understand how they can compare and evaluate claims of the past, not necessarily to determine a definitive 'truth,' but to begin to appreciate how the validity of claims about the past are assessed (Chapman, 2011).

Through your curriculum, you should address common misconceptions that arise regarding disciplinary practices. For example, it is common for pupils (and adults) to see historians as chroniclers of historical facts. Pupils may perceive history as a 'fact-finding' mission where the discovery of a single document or artefact may reveal one true account of the past. These types of misconceptions can be further embedded by lessons that require pupils to act like 'detectives' trying to solve mysteries of the past or tasks that encourage pupils to be 'mini-historians' and make their own historical judgments without sufficient knowledge. These types of lessons deepen misconceptions by misrepresenting the highly complex nature of historical practices. While it is unlikely that pupils will master a sophisticated understanding of disciplinary knowledge by the end of primary school, you should avoid embedding misconceptions like this and focus on laying the foundations for deep understanding through meaningful examples that accurately represent disciplinary knowledge in context. Reframing how you talk in history can help with this. For example, using phrases such as these can support pupils build an understanding of the discipline:

- 'We know about X because of Y.'

- 'Historians aren't certain, but many have argued that…'

- 'Some historians have argued that X can be used as evidence to show Y.'

- 'Some historians have argued X, while others have argued Y.'

Disciplinary knowledge should not be taught separately from substantive knowledge, as pupils require secure historical knowledge to make sense of it in practice. The best way to do this is to weave disciplinary knowledge into each topic you teach, enabling pupils to build on this knowledge over time. In Chapter 5, we will look at examples of how you can do this in practice.

Arguably, teaching pupils disciplinary knowledge in history not only provides them with a solid foundation for secondary history education but also gives them the tools needed to navigate modern life (Tunzelmann, 2021). In fact, it is hard to think of a discipline more well-suited to empowering pupils to think critically and question our modern, information-heavy world than history.

Disciplinary concepts

Like substantive concepts, disciplinary concepts are also highly abstract. They are sometimes called 'second-order' or 'historical concepts' and they provide a common language for teachers to discuss and develop knowledge in history.

The core disciplinary concepts outlined in the National Curriculum in England and used by history teachers today are:

- Cause

- Consequence

- Continuity and change

- Similarity and difference

- Historical significance

} These concepts classify the **types of arguments** taught

- Sources and evidence

- Historical interpretations

} These are the **processes** by which evidence is established and accounts are constructed

As a subject leader, it is important to consider how to embed disciplinary concepts in your school as they frame the way we ask questions and argue about the past. In Chapter 5, we will explore how you can do this in practice in more detail.

Here is a summary of each disciplinary concept.

Cause

In history, one type of question you might try to answer relates to *why* something in the past might have happened. These sorts of questions include (but are not limited to):

- Why did X happen?
- What happened to bring about X?
- What part did X play in bringing about Y?
- Why did X happen *at this time*?
- Why did X happen *so quickly*?
- Why did X spread *so far*?

When we answer questions like these, we are looking to identify and explain the *causes* of events or situations in the past. By doing this, we form a 'causal explanation'. A causal explanation can also be referred to as a 'causal argument'. These terms can be used interchangeably because historians always form an argument when explaining why an event or situation occurred (Historical Association, 2019). When you teach children about causal explanations, you show them how to argue in a specific way. You can do this by providing multiple opportunities for children to both listen to and read examples of causal explanations and have a go at practising them themselves, both orally and in writing. You can explicitly introduce children to these forms of arguments through the questions you ask, as we will look at in more depth in Chapter 5. Through repeated encounters over time with these types of questions, children will be able to develop a deeper understanding of the complex ways historians build causal arguments (Ofsted, 2021).

Here are some examples of causation questions in the primary curriculum:

KEY STAGE	CAUSATION QUESTION
KS1	What caused the Great Fire of London to spread so quickly?
LKS2	Why did the Western Roman Empire collapse in the fifth century?
UKS2	What led to the Bristol Bus Boycott?

Consequence

When we answer questions about consequences, we explore the relationship between an event or development and what happened after as a result. Navey has referred to this as studying the 'outworking' of a particular event or development (Navey, 2018). Questions exploring consequences are less frequently used than those focused on causation. In fact, at the Historical Association Conference in 2012, Fordham described consequence as 'causation's forgotten sibling' (Historical Association, 2021). The main reason for this is that a significant amount of knowledge is required to attempt a question that analyses the consequences of an event or development. To do this well, pupils not only need to know a lot about the event or development itself but also about what life was like both *before* and *after* the event took place to be able to reflect on the significance of its impact. Additionally, the impact of some aspects of history can be felt long after the initial development took place and could be ongoing. For example, you could argue that the impact of the British Industrial Revolution is still being experienced today. Therefore, it is a good idea to set the parameters of the scale and scope of the consequences being explored when answering these types of questions. For example, to focus on the consequences of the Industrial Revolutions in Britain from 1760–1900.

Here are some examples of consequence questions in the primary curriculum:

KEY STAGE	CONSEQUENCE QUESTION
KS1	What happened when Rosa Parks refused to give up her seat on the bus?
LKS2	To what extent did the Romans improve life in England?
UKS2	What impact did WWI have on Britain between 1918 and 1939?

Continuity and change

Questions relating to 'continuity and change' teach children about the important process of change. When understanding change, we want children to begin to grasp that some changes may appear ongoing, gradual and evolutionary, whereas others may be more abrupt or revolutionary (Shemilt, 1980). We also want to help children begin to understand that in history, we see uneven rates of change and continuities and that change does not necessarily mean progress.

Questions related to change could focus on identifying the nature, extent or pace of change. For example:

- What change has occurred?
- What stayed the same?
- What kind of change was this?
- How significant were these changes?
- How quickly did the change happen?
- How extensive were the changes?

When you discuss continuities and change, you may wish to look at both the wider-scale changes that occurred at a national or global level, as well as introducing children to smaller-scale 'micro-histories' that explore how these changes were experienced by individuals living at the time. For example, you may discuss the extent to which the Industrial Revolution significantly changed the way people lived and worked in the nineteenth century by focusing on some local stories from people living at the time. You could also look at more general aspects of change, such as the growth of factories and the introduction of the railways.

Here are some examples of continuity and change questions in the primary curriculum:

KEY STAGE	CONTINUITY AND CHANGE QUESTION
KS1	How has our local area changed over time?
LKS2	To what extent did life in Britain change between the Stone Age and the Iron Age?
UKS2	To what extent did life in Britain change drastically between 450 and 1066?

Similarity and difference

The concept of 'similarity and difference' is closely related to the ideas of generalisation and diversity. When we answer questions related to similarities and differences, we consider to what extent we can make generalisations about the past. This concept is not concerned with explaining what is similar/different about the past and today – those types of questions are related to change. Questions pertaining to similarity and difference require children to consider how historians group people, situations, and structures and ask them to evaluate how accurate these groupings are. For example, we may consider all citizens living in ancient Athens to be 'Athenians', but to what extent did all people living in Athens have similar experiences? Therefore, we can explore this concept by analysing the similarities and differences between different groups of people (such as the rich and the poor, or men and women) living in the same period. By doing this, we support pupils with understanding that while generalisations are powerful tools in history, historians have to consider their limitations in capturing the full complexity of the past (Ofsted, 2021).

As a history subject leader, you may wish to think about how you teach this concept in your school by first thinking about the different historical categories that you introduce children to through your curriculum. Some of these categories may be more generalised and used across a number of topics, such as categories related to:

- **gender**: men, women
- **roles:** merchants, priests, farmers
- **religious beliefs**: Catholics, Protestants, Jews
- **economic or political status:** ruling class, working class, barons, peasants.

Others may be period-specific, for example, 'suffragettes' and 'suffragists'. When we study history, we use these categories to compare the experiences of people within different categories and the experiences of people within the same categories to provide a more nuanced understanding of the past.

The concept of 'similarity and difference' is important for challenging generalisations and helping pupils understand the diversity of the human experience. Through engaging in these questions, pupils will begin to recognise that while generalisations are important in history, they must always be open for discussion.

Here are some examples of 'similarity and difference' questions in the primary curriculum:

KEY STAGE	SIMILARITY AND DIFFERENCE QUESTION
KS1	What was life like for people living in Tudor England?
LKS2	To what extent were the experiences of people living in ancient Greece the same?
UKS2	To what extent did the Industrial Revolution change the lives of all people in Britain in the eighteenth century?

Historical significance

To grapple with the concept of 'historical significance' we first need to consider *what history is*. As discussed in Chapter 1, history is not the past. The past consists of every single action, person, achievement or atrocity that has existed or occurred before now. The past is so 'mind-bogglingly vast' that the stories that we could tell about it are infinite (Historical Association, 2020b). However, only a small fraction of the past becomes *history*. History is forced to operate on the basis that some things are more important than others. Both consciously and unconsciously, choices are made individually and as a society, when history is written. When we explore 'historical significance' we are considering why and how this happens.

Aspects of the past that get talked about, recorded and written about have been considered *significant* by certain people. Things that have not been talked about, recorded and written about can be thought of as *silences*. It is through the process of history-making that historical significance arises. It is important that children understand that historical significance is not fixed. Over time, as historians ask new questions about the past, they seek to amplify the voices of the 'silenced'. Some things might be seen as significant at the time but less so later on. Whereas other aspects of the past may be valued as significant long after they took place. Different people will hold different viewpoints about what they view as significant.

Research has shown that many children struggle to grasp the concept of historical significance and how it is ascribed (Wrenn, 2011). One of the hardest parts about teaching historical significance is ensuring that children begin to understand that historical significance is not attached to the event, person or situation and is ever-shifting. One practical way to help pupils grapple with this concept is to construct a criterion to support thinking and discussions, just as secondary teachers Phillips and Counsell did in their classrooms (Phillips, 2002, and Counsell, 2005). For example, if you were teaching pupils about the Norman Conquest, you could ask children to consider the following criteria:

- **Remembered:** how and why is the Normal Conquest remembered by people today?
- **Impact:** what changed as a result of the Norman Conquest?
- **Revealing:** what can the Norman Conquest reveal about life at this time?

Our aim as primary history teachers should be to begin to get our children to notice and think about how some aspects of the past receive attention and others do not. One way we can do this is by recognising the significance of what we are teaching and highlighting this during our lessons. For example, you could introduce a new topic by emphasising how incredible it is that hundreds, or even thousands of years ago, something happened that has been talked about by so many people that we are now here learning about it today! The fact that any event, development or person is in your curriculum means that it has most likely been ascribed historical significance, so you have lots of opportunities to discuss this with the children.

Here are some examples of 'historical significance' questions in the primary curriculum:

KEY STAGE	HISTORICAL SIGNIFICANCE QUESTION
KS1	Why do historians think that X is a significant person to learn about?
LKS2	What was remarkable about the discovery of Tutankhamun's tomb?
UKS2	How significant was the reign of Queen Victoria?

Sources and evidence

When you look at 'sources and evidence' in the primary classroom, you are providing a 'hands-on' introduction to how the discipline works. Through engaging with sources in your lessons, children will begin to understand that there would be no history without having access to the 'records and relics' of the past (Ashby, 2011). One of the most important things you need to remember when teaching about 'sources and evidence' is that these words should not be used interchangeably. They do not mean the same thing. Sources are like the 'raw ingredients', which on their own cannot *tell us* anything as they cannot speak for themselves (Ashby, 2011). Historians use sources as evidence to back up their claims. Therefore, sources can only yield evidence when they are used by historians.

One of the important ideas that pupils need to understand about sources and evidence is that history is written based on partial records and relics. A common misconception that pupils might hold is that all the information historians need is out there and a historian's job is to find the missing puzzle pieces to create a true account of the past. This misconception can be embedded further if teachers ask children to use sources as part of a 'fact-finding mission' or present children with a mystery to be solved using 'clues from the past'. Instead, teachers should explicitly teach children about how sources can be used, ensuring they have the contextual background knowledge to access a source before letting them have a go at engaging with it. For example, if you want to look at a portrait of a significant monarch, it is best if the children have some prior knowledge of the person and the period so that they can engage more deeply with the source and have richer discussions about how historians could use it.

Another common misconception that pupils often develop is that some sources hold intrinsic reliability, whereas others should be written off as 'biased' (Lang, 1993). LeCocq shows how we can address this notion of 'bias' being bad by deliberatively studying what we can learn from an author's 'biases' (LeCocq, 2000). By doing this, we can explicitly demonstrate that while some sources may be unreliable for presenting us with the facts of an event or period, they can be highly useful in showing us what people in the past thought and believed.

When using sources with children, we can ask them questions such as:

- What does it say?
- What is it about?
- Who wrote it?
- Why do you think it was written?
- What was the purpose of this record at the time?
- Who was it written for?
- Are the authors of this source in a position to know what they claim?

In Chapter 5, we will look in more depth at how we can introduce children to sources.

Here are some examples of questions relating to 'sources and evidence' in the primary curriculum:

KEY STAGE	SOURCES AND EVIDENCE QUESTIONS
KS1	What can we learn about (insert your town/village) in X (insert time period of study) from what has been left behind?
LKS2	How much can the Anglo-Saxon Chronicle tell us about life in Anglo-Saxon England?
UKS2	How can we know about life in Roman Britain?

Historical interpretation

When we consider historical interpretations, we are looking at the ways in which the past has been interpreted or represented. Writing history always involves careful selection of 'evidence' and interpretations – no historian can write history exactly as it was (Carr and Lipscombe, 2021). We want our pupils to begin to understand that historical interpretations are more like theories in response to a question or problem rather than facts. History is always authored which means that historical interpretations are influenced by the thoughts and experiences of those who wrote them. Interpretations change over time, and historians respond and review the historical interpretations of others. If we want our pupils to engage with the discipline of history fully, it is vital that we introduce them to a wide variety of interpretations and make them the main focus of some of our lessons. Asking pupils to think like historians without having access to historical interpretations is like asking someone to compose music without listening to any (Historical Association, 2019a).

When teaching about interpretations, you can make them the focus of one lesson or the focus of a series of lessons.

Here are some examples of questions relating to interpretation that we might ask in the primary curriculum:

KEY STAGE	INTERPRETATION QUESTION
UKS2	Why have historians X and Y disagreed about the causes of World War II?

Chapter summary

- Substantive knowledge in history refers to *knowledge of the past*.

- Disciplinary knowledge refers to *knowledge of the discipline* of history.

- Substantive concepts are concepts that are concerned with the substantive content of the history being studied, such as 'democracy', 'empire', and 'invasion'.

- Disciplinary concepts are concepts that relate to the discipline of history.

- The key disciplinary concepts teachers should teach in history are cause, consequence, similarity and difference, continuity and change, historical significance, sources and evidence, and historical interpretations.

Questions for reflection

- What is the difference between substantive and disciplinary knowledge?
- Why are substantive concepts important in history, and how do I embed them in our curriculum?
- How do I develop disciplinary knowledge in history in our school?

Example PD session: substantive and disciplinary knowledge

Here is an example of what a PD session on substantive and disciplinary knowledge could look like:

TIMING SUGGESTION	SESSION GUIDANCE
15 mins	Using the 'What's the wisdom on' articles (see below) and the information in this chapter, explain what is meant by: • substantive knowledge • disciplinary knowledge • substantive concepts • disciplinary concepts.
25 mins	Take an example from your curriculum and model identifying the key substantive and disciplinary knowledge being taught, and how you might teach this in your class. Ask teachers to look at their next history unit and ask them to identify: • the key substantive knowledge • how disciplinary knowledge will be embedded • what substantive concepts are being taught.
5 mins	Provide teachers with a poster that defines substantive and disciplinary knowledge to have in their classroom to support them while teaching history.

Explore further

- The Historical Association have a 'What's the wisdom on' feature that provides short guides to aspects of teaching history, including the disciplinary concepts discussed in this chapter. It can be viewed here: https://www.history.org.uk/publications/categories/8/module/8697/teaching-history-regular-features/9356/whats-the-wisdom-on
- *Debates in History Teaching*, 2nd edition (2017) edited by Ian Davies
- Ofsted's 'Research Review Series: History' (2021), available here: https://www.gov.uk/government/publications/research-review-series-history

4 Curriculum design

Curriculum is not one aspect of education: it is education (Howard and Hill, 2020). Therefore, this chapter is arguably the most important one in the book! Following on from Chapter 3, we will now look in more detail at the curriculum choices you need to make when you are developing or reviewing your history curriculum. This chapter is divided into four sections:

1. Deciding what to teach
2. Sequencing the curriculum
3. Curriculum as a narrative
4. How to get started with developing the curriculum

Within each section, we will examine both the theory and research, as well as practical solutions and ideas, to support you with engaging deeply in effective curriculum design.

1. Deciding what to teach

The first aspect of curriculum design is deciding what to teach. As primary teachers, you have a great deal of freedom when it comes to making this decision. Although (in England) you have to follow the National Curriculum, this still leaves you with a lot of decision-making power regarding exactly what you include in your school's curriculum. As we discussed in Chapter 1, you need to have clear aims for history in your school. What you choose to teach should be influenced by these aims. However, the main aim of your history curriculum should be to enable your pupils to develop a deep understanding and appreciation of the discipline of history. So, how exactly can you do this?

Substantive knowledge

Firstly, you need to ensure that your curriculum supports your pupils to 'build a body of substantive historical knowledge' (Hammond, 2014). As discussed in Chapter 3, developing substantive knowledge, or 'knowledge *of the past*', is essential in enabling pupils to interpret, understand and question everything they learn in history. As a subject leader, you need to reflect on *what* substantive knowledge you choose to teach and why. Therefore, you need to wrestle with important questions when designing or reviewing the content in your curriculum, such as:

- Which people, events, and developments do you teach and why?
- Which time periods and geographical locations do you cover in your curriculum and why?
- What do you want children to take away from this unit?
- How will learning this support pupils with accessing the curriculum later on?

When you make these important choices, you need to consider what the 'opportunity cost' is for each decision you make. You only have time in your curriculum to include a tiny amount of everything that happened in the past. Everything else has to be excluded. Therefore, you must also ask yourself:

- What have you decided to leave out and why?
- Why do you teach this over that?
- Why has this 'made the cut' in your curriculum?

This can seem like a daunting task, so it can be useful to consider a criterion to help you decide what to teach and what to leave out.

For example:

1. **Profound**: How profound was this event, or development, in changing people's lives? How many people were affected? How long-term were the effects?

2. **Ambitious**: How will learning this challenge pupils? Is this something that children are likely to learn at home? Will learning this provide a good foundation for success in Key Stage 3 and beyond?

3. **Relevant:** How relevant is this to the lives of pupils today? How can it help them make sense of the modern world? Does studying this present opportunities for children to engage with local history?

4. **Interesting:** Is this interesting? How will learning this engage pupils and foster a love and appreciation of history?

5. **Significant:** How historically significant is this person, event, or development, and why?

This does not mean that everything you choose to teach needs to be really 'profound' or that we should only teach things we view as 'relevant' to pupils today. Instead, you can view a criterion like this as a tool for supporting you with having important conversations about what you choose to include and exclude from the curriculum.

Powerful knowledge

When it comes to making those important decisions regarding curriculum content, you may have heard the famous saying from Mathew Arnold that we should aim to teach 'the best that's been thought and said' (Arnold, 1869). While Arnold was deeply committed to education for all, the concept of teaching 'the best' has been seen by some as controversial and elitist. However, while it is probably impossible to curate the very 'best' history curriculum, there certainly are 'better' (and worse) ways of doing it.

Young and Lambert argue for the concept of 'better knowledge' (Young and Lambert, 2014). 'Better knowledge' is the best knowledge available in the discipline and the best means we currently have for creating new knowledge. In their book, *Knowledge and the Future School*, Young and Lambert argue that the purpose of schools should be to teach children this 'better knowledge' – knowledge that takes children beyond their everyday experiences – to help them make sense of the world. In order to specify 'better knowledge', Young and Lambert came up with the idea of 'powerful knowledge' as a driving principle for curriculum development (Young and Lambert, 2014). 'Powerful knowledge' is knowledge which is:

- **distinct from 'common-sense' knowledge** that we gain from everyday experiences.
- **systematic:** this means that it can form the basis for generalisations and making connections beyond specific contexts. For example, in history we might teach the concept of 'empire', which could support making generalisations and could be applied in multiple contexts across our curriculum.
- **specialised**: this means that the knowledge has been developed by experts in the field. In our subject, this would mean academic historians.

Therefore, another tool for thinking about what to include in your curriculum is the concept of 'powerful knowledge'.

Core and hinterland knowledge

The idea of 'core' and 'hinterland' knowledge is another useful way of thinking about curriculum content (Counsell, 2018). 'Core knowledge' is what you want pupils to retain in their long-term memory. It is the 'residue' that is left, the headlines and the key points that you want children to take with them to secondary and beyond. The 'hinterland' refers to the details, rich narratives, metaphors, elaborations, and embellishments that we use to 'furnish and frame the core' (Howard and Hill, 2020). Counsell argues that while the 'hinterland' is the feeder or supporter of the core when it comes to the curriculum, it is just as important (Counsell, 2018). For example, if you are teaching about World War I, the 'core' might be to understand how the war was fought, e.g. at sea, on land, and in the air. However, simply telling children this is unlikely to lead to long-term learning. If we want them to fully understand and remember the ways in which the war was fought, we need to provide rich examples, pictures, stories of battles and first-hand accounts from soldiers. All this 'hinterland' knowledge does not need to be remembered in the long term, e.g. we will not expect children to remember the name of a soldier and the exact date of each battle studied, but it is essential as it ensures that the children understand the 'core.'

Therefore, when you are having conversations about curriculum content, you can identify the 'core' knowledge you want children to retain in their long-term memories and the 'hinterland' that will provide the backdrop to the core. It is important to note that the 'hinterland' should support the 'core' rather than distract from it. For example, using the story of the discovery of Tutankhamun's tomb could help children understand more about both life in ancient Egypt and archaeological discoveries. Whereas activities such as 'designing your own tomb' or 'building a pyramid' distract from this learning rather than adding to the 'core'. Therefore, when designing your curriculum, you can ask yourself, 'Is this useful hinterland knowledge that adds context, or could this distract from the core?'

Breadth vs depth

Another area we need to 'wrestle with' when deciding what to teach is the interplay between outline and depth (Byrom and Riley, 2008). Often in schools, we are told that we should be doing fewer things in greater depth. You may have heard people arguing that the curriculum is too broad and that we should focus on mastering aspects in more depth rather than teaching a little about a lot. While this argument may be valid in some subjects, you should be wary of this approach in history. The reason for this is that you cannot fully understand specific aspects of the past without understanding the broader historical context in which they sit. Jenkins has argued that depth should follow breadth in history because, without an awareness of the broader timeline, history becomes meaningless (Jenkins, 2018). You can ensure that you teach broader outlines by:

- placing British history into a wider global context.
- placing an event, development, or period within a wider chronological framework.
- teaching about the broader social, cultural, political, or religious context that this aspect, event, or development sits within (Riley, 1997).

For example, if I was teaching children about the Romans in Britain, rather than focusing on one aspect in depth (such as Hadrian's wall), I could begin the unit by introducing children to the broader Roman Empire first, looking at how it was established, who the Romans were, how their army was organised, where the empire stretched to, and place the invasion of Britain on a timeline. Once the children have developed a broader understanding of the Romans, I could move on to looking at a particular aspect in more depth, such as a local Roman archaeological discovery. Teaching overviews could be one aspect of one lesson or take up a whole lesson or a series of lessons. This is another decision you need to consider when you are designing your curriculum.

Local history

You also need to consider what local histories will be included as part of your curriculum. Local history is a fascinating way of introducing children to the discipline of history through the rich stories that took place on their doorstep. It can be challenging for young children to imagine that the place they live now looked different in the past. To help children see beyond their experiences, It is a good idea to consider using images, reconstructions, photographs and paintings to help them imagine the past. Rather than seeing a local study as a separate aspect of our curriculum, it is a good idea to consider how local history fits in with wider historical narratives (as we will discuss when considering sequencing).

Diversity

In addition to considering local content, you should make sure that your curriculum looks beyond your doorsteps and includes geographically diverse aspects of the past. You should aim to ensure that you are teaching the history of humanity rather than the history of a small group of people. Building on Rudine Sims Bishop's work, Adcock argues that your curriculum should be both a 'window and a mirror' (Adcock, 2021). The mirror signifies that all pupils should be able to see themselves in the curriculum. The window represents how your curriculum shows children the world beyond their own experience. Therefore, when selecting content for your curriculum, you should consider how you represent the diverse backgrounds of the children in your school, your local community and Britain today.

When curating a diverse curriculum, you should consider the following:

- ethnic communities
- gender
- class
- localities
- cultures
- religious perspectives
- disabilities.

It is essential that your curriculum is broad and diverse. Our history is not fixed within the boundaries of one nation and certainly does not belong to one group or society. Humans have moved around our world for thousands of years. Our cultures are intertwined, as is our history. We need to remember this when deciding what to teach our children.

Disciplinary knowledge

As discussed in Chapter 3, as well as teaching substantive knowledge, your curriculum should also enable pupils to build disciplinary knowledge – *knowledge of the discipline*. While disciplinary knowledge should not drive content decisions, you should consider how you will incorporate the disciplinary lens through each topic you plan to teach when designing your curriculum. This is discussed in more detail in Chapter 5.

2. Sequencing the curriculum

Curriculum design is all about choice. In addition to choosing what to teach, you also need to consider the order in which things are taught. Sequencing a curriculum in an intelligent and orderly way requires you to take a whole-school approach to curriculum design. Unfortunately, some schools still opt for a 'liquorice all sorts' model, where each teacher 'puts in their hand and pulls out whatever they want', creating a curriculum comprised of a series of stand-alone units of work (Robinson, 2022). A curriculum built in a haphazard way like this can disadvantage children – especially those who come to school with less background knowledge – by not providing firm foundations for them to build on knowledge over time.

Unlike subjects like science and maths, where content is organised more hierarchically, knowledge in history can be built horizontally and cumulatively (Bernstein, 2000). Theoretically, two pupils could attain equally well despite studying different curriculum models (Counsell, 2021). However, this does not mean that any sequence will do. You need to ensure that your curriculum is well sequenced so that children create a coherent 'big picture' or mental framework of the past and can connect new learning with existing knowledge. Without careful consideration of sequence, you risk children's knowledge of the past becoming 'episodic, romanticised and ultimately meaningless' (Morton, 2000). This is why coherence matters. According to Myatt, a 'bitty' curriculum lacking a coherent sequence means that fragments of unconnected knowledge are left floating around without being placed into a 'bigger basket' of understanding (Myatt, 2018). A curriculum becomes coherently sequenced when you can combine what you learn into a bigger narrative.

Sequencing and findings from cognitive science

Research from cognitive science helps us to understand why it is important to sequence your curriculum carefully. Bartlett's schema theory explains how new knowledge must fit in with what is already known to be understood (Bartlett, 1932). Therefore, if you do not consider the sequence of the curriculum, some children may lack the background knowledge needed to understand new content.

Sweller's cognitive load theory argues that activating prior knowledge reduces the extraneous cognitive load on working memory, freeing it to focus and make connections with new material (Sweller, 2012). Therefore, by ensuring that pupils meaningfully build on knowledge over time, cognitive load is reduced, enabling pupils to process and retain new content. Further research by Bransford, Brown and Cocking has shown that when pupils use prior knowledge to make sense of new content, it makes learning easier to comprehend and remember (Bransford et al., 2000).

Furthermore, as Ebbinghaus first demonstrated in 1885 with his 'forgetting curve,' spacing out learning over time leads to long-term learning (Ebbinghaus, 1885). Research in the field of neuroscience continues to support the practice of spacing out content to reduce cognitive load and improve long-term retention (Sisti et al., 2007). So, how can you do this with your history curriculum?

Chronological understanding

A history curriculum can support learning over time by drawing threads between overarching ideas and supporting pupils with relating new content with existing background knowledge. In history, we have the chronological axis, which can support us with this. Events that take place across time and place relate to one another, and by building chronological knowledge and understanding through the curriculum, you can support pupils by revisiting and making connections between people, events, and developments in the past.

This does not mean that your curriculum has to be sequenced chronologically. Although there may be some benefits to studying some aspects of the past chronologically, your curriculum can move back and forth in time and still build chronological understanding if you reinforce how aspects of the past fit chronologically with previously studied content. For example, when learning about the Stone Age to the Iron Age, you could make connections between what pupils learned about the ancient Egyptians living during the same period, and what you have already learned about Romans in Britain, which happened after this period.

Most people would agree that building chronological understanding should be an important aim of a history curriculum. But to do this well, you need to appreciate the complexity of what you are requiring from children. Chronological understanding requires more than an ability to place events in order. Understanding chronology in history is also underpinned by several mathematical concepts, such as place value, negative numbers and measurement, as well as developing a sense of:

- **scale**, e.g. exactly how long ago was the prehistoric period in relation to the Tudors?
- **period**, e.g. exactly what is conjured up by the expression 'Tudor England'?
- **frameworks of the past**, e.g. building coherent narrative frameworks of history (as discussed below) (Dawson, 2004).

3. Curriculum as a narrative

As well as structuring the curriculum to support pupils in acquiring a basic chronological understanding of the past, you can use the chronological axis to support pupils with understanding significant phases of human development and sow the seeds of coherent historical narratives (Shemilt, 2000). As we will discuss in Chapter 6, narratives are fundamental to the discipline of history. Counsell describes the curriculum as 'content structured as a narrative over time' (Counsell, 2018). Therefore, your history curriculum can be viewed as a narrative, with each part of the curriculum supporting pupils to make deeper connections over time.

The nature of the discipline of history supports you in building your curriculum narrative, as stories of the past are all connected across time and place. This is because everything that happened is intertwined and related to what came before. Significant events rarely, if ever, occur in isolation. The curriculum should reveal more about the past with each story it tells, supporting pupils to understand how layers of historical knowledge connect and interact. Therefore, each topic you teach should not be viewed as a single story but just part of the broader story of the history of humanity. These stories stretch through time and help children make sense of new content by framing it in an unfolding picture (Corfield, 2009). When you view curriculum as a narrative, you see that each episode enables pupils to understand more over time. Some stories are better understood when studied first, while others make more sense later on. Each part of the curriculum paves the way for the next.

Through a well-sequenced curriculum, you can unfold stories over time that span thousands of years to develop a deeper understanding of human history and the world we live in today. Therefore, your curriculum needs to take the long view and teach history as a whole narrative rather than selected fragments of unrelated stories (Shemilt, 2000).

So, what does this look like in practice?

Case study: building broader historical narratives

Nadia is an experienced subject leader responsible for history across her trust's three primary schools. She has recently read *The Caliph's Coin* by Shemilt (2000) and has reflected upon her trust's history curriculum. Following pupil voice interviews in her three schools, she realises that children cannot always make connections between the topics they study. She decides to review the curriculum and develop teachers to ensure children are supported in building broader historical narratives. She chooses to focus on three core narratives:

- **'The story of politics and power'**: Who has power, and what do they do with it? How is power distributed, and how does this change over time? Who is excluded from power?

- **'The story of society, culture and religion'**: What was it like to live during this period, and how does this change over time? How was society structured? What did people believe in, and how did this impact their lives?

- **'The story of industry, technology and production'**: How have technological developments changed how humans live their lives over time? How are goods and food produced and traded? Who is involved? What has been the impact of advancements in industry and technology over time?

While she recognises that these aspects are interconnected, she considers them to be three core narrative frameworks that connect many aspects of their curriculum. To support teachers in understanding this, she holds a staff meeting where she shares her ideas, and they spend time in their key stages highlighting where they teach aspects of these narratives. Nadia captures their discussions in a document she shares with all teachers in the trust. An example is given in the following 'In practice' feature.

LEARNING	
EYFS	Children engage in a topic called 'Kings and Queens.' They dress up in costumes in the role-play area and listen to stories about fascinating kings and queens in the past, such as King John and Elizabeth I. They are introduced to key vocabulary such as 'king,' 'queen,' 'monarch,' 'crown,' 'throne', and 'royal.'
KS1	Children learn more about kings and queens when they compare Elizabeth I and Queen Victoria. They build on their knowledge from the EYFS to look at how the throne was passed down in royal families and look at family trees. They are introduced to the idea of democracy when they look at local MPs.
KS2	Children learn how power is distributed in Britain from earliest times to today, including Iron Age tribes, the invading Roman Empire, Anglo-Saxon and Viking rule, the first king of England, King John and the Magna Carta, and the Glorious Revolution. The children also develop their knowledge of democracy when they study the ancient Greeks and the Suffragettes. Furthermore, they consider power and politics when they study global history units, including ancient Egyptian pharaohs and Alexander the Great's empire, when they look at the ancient Greeks.

Making connections

When sequencing your curriculum, you should also consider how learning new content fits with what children have learned across the wider curriculum. This way, you can support pupils with applying their background knowledge across disciplines in meaningful ways. You should start by considering what important pre-requisite knowledge is needed at each stage of the curriculum and make links within and across the subjects. For example, before learning about the Vikings, it would be beneficial for children to understand what life was like in Britain prior to their arrival. It would also be useful for children to have locational knowledge of Northern Europe and the British Isles, an understanding of 'settlement', 'migration', and 'trade', and know a little about Christianity. Retrieving this prior knowledge when learning about the Vikings will support pupils in understanding and remembering more of the new content being taught, securing a more detailed historical narrative of this period.

In the curriculum, this could look like this:

STAGE	WHAT CHILDREN ARE TAUGHT ABOUT
EYFS	Children are taught about: • where they live and introduced to the countries in the UK • what a map is • basic things that humans need to live, e.g. fresh water and food • Christianity in the context of celebrations such as Easter and Christmas.
KS1	Children are taught about: • the four countries in the UK in geography • what it means to be 'Christian' and some Christian beliefs in RE • Europe, including Northern Europe in geography.
KS2	Children are taught about: • Christianity in more depth in RE • what a 'settlement' is, 'trade' and 'migration' in geography • the Stone Age to the Iron Age and the Romans in Britain – building a picture of life in Britain before the Anglo-Saxons arrived in history.
	When they are taught about Anglo-Saxon Britain and the Vikings later in KS2, they are able to make connections and relate prior knowledge to support their understanding of new content.

4. How to get started with developing the curriculum

As a history subject leader, you may be responsible for developing the curriculum in your school, or this might be something that has already been established for you. Whether you design your own curriculum or embed and enact one designed elsewhere, it is important that you know what is taught across the school and understand how and why it has been sequenced in this way. How schools establish their history curriculum varies greatly from school to school. In some academies, the curriculum is designed by a centralised team. While in other schools, the curriculum may be adopted from other schools, or teachers may be asked to follow a scheme.

If you are following a curriculum that you were not involved in designing, you need to reflect upon what we have discussed in this chapter and review how well your curriculum is meeting the needs of your children. For example, you may wish to look in depth at how your local history fits in with the scheme you are following.

If your school decides to create its own curriculum, then it is best to think about how you will ensure that you utilise the best expertise available to create a curriculum that is ambitious and well-sequenced. Therefore, you need to consider everything we have learned so far about how you can select and sequence knowledge in history. As we have discussed, history is different from other subjects, like science and maths, and therefore, we should resist generic approaches to curriculum design. In history, we have to consider:

- powerful knowledge
- core and hinterland knowledge
- chronology
- narrative
- local, national, and global elements
- depth and breadth
- diversity
- disciplinary knowledge of history.

This can feel like a lot to think about, so it is important that you remember that you do not have to do everything yourself. The National Curriculum in England provides some guidance on what to teach to get you started, and you can use subject associations, such as the Historical Association, and share best practices with colleagues in other schools. Therefore, the next thing to consider when designing or reviewing your curriculum is *who* will be involved.

The curriculum team

Developing your history curriculum should not be the sole responsibility of one person. If you want to curate a rich, ambitious, and well-sequenced curriculum, you should consider the questions below.

- Who will be involved in designing your curriculum?
- What help might you need?
- What expertise do you have in your school, and how could you develop this further?
- Who could help you review your choices?

- Are there any teachers in other schools or trusts that could support you with this?
- Do you need to utilise expertise from a subject association or another curriculum expert?
- Could you work with your local secondary school to enhance your curriculum?

Stenhouse argues that there is no curriculum development without teacher development (Stenhouse, 1975). Therefore, designing or reviewing your curriculum is a great way of developing professional knowledge. However, while you must listen to and involve teachers in ongoing curriculum discussions, you should be cautious of involving too many voices in the initial stages of curriculum design as this can make decision-making difficult. It might be worth appointing someone with expertise (perhaps yourself) to make the final decisions. As we stated at the start of this chapter, you have so many possible choices to make in history, it is best if these decisions are made by people with the deepest understanding of the discipline.

This also means you should be cautious when involving children and parents or carers in curriculum decisions. While you certainly should listen to their questions or suggestions, you must ensure your curriculum is developed by experts with the subject and pedagogical knowledge needed to make these tough decisions.

Time

In addition to considering who is involved in your curriculum team, you also need to consider how much time you have to dedicate to curriculum development. Curriculum work is not easy or quick, and you need to have the time to think about and discuss the important decisions you need to make. Unfortunately, time is something that we always need more of in primary schools! Therefore, you need to be realistic when you set out this work. Suppose you have not been allocated very much time for curriculum development. In that case, it might be a good idea to consider working with colleagues in another school and sharing resources or adopting and adapting an existing scheme. If you are fortunate enough to be given time and resources to complete this task, remember that curriculum design cannot happen in a day (despite what some consultants might tell you!) and devise a plan outlining what you wish to achieve and by when. You also need to remember that curriculum development should be ongoing. Ideally, our schools should foster an environment where these deep discussions are given the time and space to thrive so that we can offer all children a rich and well-sequenced curriculum.

Topics or discrete lessons

Another decision you need to make when designing your curriculum is whether history will be taught through a 'topic' or as a discrete subject. A 'topic', sometimes called a 'theme', is a cross-curricular approach to curriculum design where instead of teaching discrete subjects, everything is taught under an umbrella heading, such as 'Under the sea' or 'Food and farming'. While a topic-based approach may enable children to make cross-curricular connections, you must be careful that your history curriculum does not get lost under a heading, as this can result in children missing out on understanding and appreciating history as a discipline. If you adopt a topic approach, when teaching elements of the topic that are history-based, it is important that children understand that they are learning history. For example, you could do this in practice by beginning the lesson by explaining to the children that today we are learning about 'history'. You also need to ensure that the history curriculum taught over time is rich and well-sequenced and that children see the connections between topics and don't just jump from topic to topic without making these connections. Curriculum design is more challenging when a school teaches history through a topic, as it is common for content to be selected to fit in with the topic rather than because of its importance for the subject. Therefore, many primary schools now teach history as a discrete subject. This is a decision that needs to be made by each school.

Codifying the curriculum

Another decision you need to make is how you will codify the curriculum. It is important that your curriculum is clearly written down so that everyone in school understands what should be taught and when. Some schools may choose to have a highly codified curriculum, with resources like slideshows and booklets. The benefit of this is that it provides clarity to teachers and helps ensure progression over time. However, a downside to having a highly codified curriculum is that it can become rigid and prevent teachers from using their professional judgement to effectively adapt the curriculum to the needs of children in their class. Therefore, it is important to think deeply about how you will codify your curriculum and why. Some of the documents you can use to codify your curriculum include:

- long-term plans, or 'curriculum overviews,' highlighting the topics or units that will be taught
- medium-term plans, with content that will be taught within each topic
- lesson plans, including key vocabulary
- a list of enrichment opportunities, e.g., trips, visitors and experiences that will be offered as part of the curriculum
- booklets
- slideshows
- assessments with clear endpoints
- knowledge organisers.

Chapter summary

- Schools have a great deal of freedom when it comes to deciding what to teach in history.
- We have explored ways of helping you make important decisions, such as using a criterion, when deciding what to teach.
- As well as deciding what to teach, you must also ensure your curriculum is well-sequenced so children can build connections over time.
- You can develop your curriculum in different ways; some schools opt to write their own, whereas others may work collaboratively with other schools or adopt and adapt a scheme.
- Curriculum work is never finished. Wherever you are on your journey, be sure to continue to review and reflect to ensure that you continue to offer your children a rich, ambitious, and well-sequenced curriculum.

Questions for reflection

- What do we choose to teach and why?
- How has our curriculum been sequenced, and why?
- How do we ensure that children develop chronological understanding across our curriculum?
- How did we get to where we are today with our curriculum?
- How could I make our curriculum even better?

Example PD session: areas for improvement

Here is an example of what a PD session on improving the history curriculum could look like.

TIMING SUGGESTION	SESSION GUIDANCE
15 mins	Before the session, reflect upon what we have discussed in this chapter and your school context. Decide upon an area you would like to improve upon, such as incorporating more diversity or local history within your curriculum. Begin your session by introducing what you have learned and why you want to improve in the area you have identified. Ensure staff are clear on how this will benefit children. For example, you could share with staff that you want to ensure the curriculum is both a 'window and a mirror' using what we have discussed in this chapter.
15 mins	In pairs or year groups, ask teachers to reflect upon the curriculum areas they teach and action plan how they could improve upon the area you have identified.
15 mins	As a school, give feedback on your discussions and begin action planning. Agree on goals and reinforce effective curriculum discussions that have taken place.

Explore further

- Christine Counsell's article 'Senior Curriculum Leadership 1: The indirect manifestation of knowledge: (A) curriculum as narrative' (2018) found here: https://thedignityofthethingblog.wordpress.com/2018/04/07/senior-curriculum-leadership-1-the-indirect-manifestation-of-knowledge-a-curriculum-as-narrative

- Denis Shemilt's article 'The Caliph's Coin: The Currency of Narrative Frameworks in History Teaching' (2000) found in *Knowing, teaching and learning in history: national and international perspectives*, by Stearns, Seixas, and Wineburg

- Michael Young and David Lambert's (2014) book *Knowledge and the Future School: Curriculum and Social Justice*

5 Historical enquiry

In this chapter, we will build on what we learned in Chapter 3 and discuss how to successfully use historical enquiries in our history lessons. The ancient Greek writer, Herodotus, thought of as the 'Father of History', laid the foundations for the methods of historical enquiry that historians still use today (Marincola, 2001). In our modern classrooms, you can introduce pupils to these methods in meaningful ways, providing them with opportunities to apply their growing knowledge, while also gaining a deeper appreciation of the discipline of history.

In this chapter, we will:

- learn what historical enquiry is and why it is important.
- identify what makes a good enquiry question.
- discuss how you can plan and teach historical enquiry in the primary classroom.
- look at a practical example of how a subject leader has embedded the use of historical enquiries in their school.

What is historical enquiry?

'Historical enquiry' describes the process that historians take to study the past. When we talk about an 'enquiry' in primary and secondary history, we are referring to a series of lessons that are connected by a focus on answering a historically-framed 'enquiry question' (Historical Association, 2020b). Over a sequence of lessons, pupils build their knowledge systematically in order to be able to answer the enquiry question at the end.

It is important that subject leaders recognise that 'historical enquiry' differs from the pedagogical approach known as enquiry-based learning. Enquiry-based learning promotes children asking their own questions and expects that they can independently research or discover new knowledge by themselves. In contrast, when engaging in a historical enquiry, questions should be planned by the teacher and the knowledge needed to adequately answer the question should be explicitly taught (Sullivan, 2018).

The power of historical enquiry lies in the steady unfolding of the question, where each lesson adds a new dimension to the child's understanding. By cumulatively building their knowledge over a series of lessons, teachers enable pupils to see new ways of answering the question. At the end of the sequence of lessons, all pupils should be empowered to formulate an argument to answer the enquiry question successfully.

Why is historical enquiry important?

As discussed in Chapter 3, progress in history is not just about securing substantive knowledge; pupils also need to develop disciplinary knowledge. Engaging in a historical enquiry is a purposeful way of weaving substantive and disciplinary knowledge together. Well-planned, historically-framed enquiry questions encourage pupils to think historically and form their arguments, using and applying their substantive knowledge to back up their points. They are also motivating as they give purpose to what the children are learning. In lessons, you can explain how what they are learning today is going to help them with answering the question later on.

Utilising the power of the enquiry question is a great way of assessing what pupils know and understand in history. We will look at this in more detail in Chapter 8. However, it is important to understand now that you do not need pupils to attempt to answer an enquiry question independently for it to be a useful tool for assessment. Even in secondary school, a historical enquiry should be teacher-led, and pupils should receive guidance, models, and support to be able to answer the question successfully.

Using historical enquiry in primary is one way you can ensure that pupils are well prepared for secondary and beyond. Through your enquiries, you are introducing children to the disciplinary practices of history, which they will engage with in more detail in Key Stage 3.

Not only do your historical enquires help build the foundation for history at secondary school, but they also prepare children for life in the modern world. It has been argued that the process of questioning and research, sifting through information, and making informed judgments provides pupils with powerful tools they need to navigate the world today (Tunzelmann, 2021). History is a way of seeing the world, and providing opportunities for children to access different viewpoints, challenge claims, understand evidence and begin to think for themselves is important to uphold a truly democratic society.

What makes a good enquiry question?

A good enquiry question needs to be precise and 'historically valid'. This means the question needs to be rooted in the practices of the discipline. When devising questions, ask yourself, 'is this the type of question that a historian might ask?' and avoid questions that require children to give a personal response, such as 'Would you have preferred to live in the Stone Age or the Iron Age?' One way you can ensure your questions are framed through a historical lens is to make sure that each question relates to one (or possibly two) disciplinary concepts that we discussed in Chapter 3.

For example:

CONCEPT	ENQUIRY QUESTION
Cause	What led to the fall of the Roman Empire?
Consequence	What impact did WWI have on Britain between 1918 and 1939?
Continuity and change	To what extent did life change in England between 450 and 1066?
Similarity and difference	To what extent were all women in Britain fighting for women's suffrage between 1830 and 1928?
Historical significance	Why is Rosa Parks still remembered today?
Sources and evidence	What can we learn about Fu Hao's life from the artefacts found in her tomb?

While you may use questions in lessons that require a descriptive response, the main enquiry question should elicit an argument so that it helps children build an understanding of how the discipline works (Riley, 2008). You should avoid asking questions with obvious answers, including any questions with yes/no answers, such as 'Did the Romans change Britain?' or 'Was Rosa Parks an important person in the civil rights movement in the USA?' These types of questions can be improved by adding statements such as '*to what extent*' or '*how far*' to ensure that the question provokes an argument.

It is also important that your questions do not require pupils to make value judgments on the past based on modern-day standards. For example, you should avoid questions such as 'Was democracy in ancient Greece fair?' or 'Did Julius Caesar deserve to die?' It is not helpful to ask children to make their own judgments about whether something was good/bad or fair/unfair based on our moral standards today, as this will lead to anachronistic judgments and could encourage children to think negatively about the people of the past.

Riley argues that a good enquiry question should also 'capture the interest and imagination of the pupils' (Riley, 2008). He argues that our questions should intrigue our pupils and provide an engaging puzzle that they can begin to solve as they progress from lesson to lesson. Therefore, your question needs to be something that is worth answering. Finally, your question needs to be something that can result in a final resolution where pupils are motivated to apply what they have learned to decisively answer the question.

Questions for teachers to consider when writing enquiry questions

- Does this question require an argument, or could it be answered with a simple 'yes/no' answer?
- Which disciplinary concept does this question relate to?
- Will children have the knowledge and/or time to be able to adequately answer this question?
- Does this question require children to make a values-based judgment?
- How will this question capture the interest of the pupils?
- Is this something that children could successfully answer?
- Is this question worth answering?

Methods of historical enquiry

As part of your history curriculum, you should aim to explicitly teach children about the methods that historians use to find out about the past. This should include how evidence is used to make historical claims, how and why contrasting arguments exist, and why different interpretations of the past have been constructed (DfE, 2013). One way you can teach this is through historical enquires. In fact, you may choose to focus the entire enquiry on sources and evidence, (such as 'What can we learn about X from what has been left behind?') or look at how and why different historical interpretations of a particular event or period exist. These types of questions teach children about the methods of historical enquiry in a purposeful and practical way.

In addition to these types of enquiries, you can also provide opportunities for children to explore a range of sources and discuss how historians use evidence within the context of other enquiry questions. For example, if you are looking at the causes of an event, you could look at relevant sources that have been used by historians as evidence.

When you plan your questions, you should think about how you might incorporate the use of appropriate sources to provide children with first-hand experience of how the discipline works. It is a good idea to utilise local archives, museums, historical associations and libraries to assist with uncovering useful sources related to your topic. Even our youngest pupils can begin to understand the methods that historians use when they are exposed to sources in a meaningful way. For example, in Key Stage 1, you could discuss with pupils how historians have been able to learn a lot about Mary Seacole from important sources, such as photographs, census returns and her autobiography.

However, teachers should be aware that it is not essential that all historical enquiries include the use of sources. While children need some understanding of how historians use sources as evidence to make and justify claims, primary pupils do not need to use sources as evidence when answering their enquiry questions (Historical Association, 2020b).

Planning for historical enquiry

An ideal time to plan for historical enquiry is at the beginning of planning a unit or topic, rather than during the unit or at the end of a series of lessons. For example, if I was planning to teach children about the Romans in Britain, I might begin by both identifying the core knowledge I want children to know (e.g. about who they were, their army, the invasion of Britain) as well as considering what enquiry question I could ask, such as 'How did the Romans conquer southern Britain so easily?', that could capture their imaginations and allow them to apply their knowledge to formulate an argument.

If you plan a unit without considering the question first, you may find that pupils are not well prepared with the knowledge they need to answer the question, or you may be limited in what you choose to ask them. However, this does not mean that everything you teach the children about the Romans has to be something that you expect them to use to answer the enquiry question. If you allow your enquiry questions to drive all your curriculum choices, you may end up narrowing your curriculum, which could result in children lacking depth of knowledge. This will be especially true if your enquiry questions are not strong enough or are focused on one specific aspect of the period. Therefore, you should expect that while some of the core knowledge you teach during your history units will be directly related to your question, other aspects of the curriculum may support pupils indirectly, for example, by helping them build a sense of the period.

Planning your question

When you plan for a historical enquiry, you may decide to introduce the question at the start of a unit or topic and support pupils to relate back and apply their new knowledge to the question during each lesson. This means that the enquiry could last a full half term, with each lesson building towards answering the question at the end. Alternatively, you could start a unit by teaching a few lessons to set the scene and build background knowledge first before introducing the enquiry question, which will be explored over the next few lessons. You need to consider how many lessons are needed to be able to answer the question sufficiently, while also recognising that dedicating too many lessons to one enquiry could limit the scope of the curriculum. For example, it is not usually advised to have one enquiry used over a 12 week term. Similarly, it is not a good idea to attempt to set a separate enquiry question for every lesson (Historical Association, 2020b). While sub-questions could be used to support children with answering the main question, pupils will not be able to gain enough knowledge to adequately answer an enquiry question in one lesson. This is why a historical enquiry should be designed to be answered across a series of lessons. While it is common for schools to do just one enquiry per topic, you could decide to do more if you feel you have sufficient time to do them well.

One of the most important aspects of planning for historical enquiry is getting the question right. As discussed above, a good enquiry question needs to be precise and historically framed. As subject leaders, we should acknowledge that writing enquiry questions requires secure subject knowledge and can be challenging to get right. Therefore, one of the best ways to support teachers with this is to collaborate and share expertise. This could be done as part of a staff training session or through collaborative planning, which could occur between teachers within your school or through teaming up with colleagues in other schools.

Another way to develop your own subject expertise is to engage with some historical scholarship and look at the types of questions that historians ask about the topics you are studying. If you don't know where to start with this, you could speak to the history department at your local secondary school or engage with the Historical Association, who provide webinars, articles and professional development to bridge the divide between academic and school history.

Local history

Another aspect to consider is how your enquiry could be enriched by incorporating local history. A question to ask yourself is, 'How did the national story play out in our local area?' For example, if you are studying a topic on important developments such as the Suffragette movement or the Industrial Revolution, think about how people in your local area were involved and how they were affected by the broader issues and events you are studying. These smaller-scale local stories can provide rich examples that can be included in the historical enquiry and help make the question feel even more relevant to the children.

Answering the question

You need to ensure that as children progress through the enquiry, each lesson reveals more and brings the children one step closer to successfully answering the question. As you plan for this, you need to be clear about *how* you will expect children to answer the enquiry question at the end and prepare them for this. The final task could require the children to respond to the question through a more traditional written response, such as an essay, or children could be required to answer in another format, such as a table, a diagram, or a 'knowledge showcase.' Alternatively, you could plan for children to answer the question orally, perhaps through a class debate or planning an assembly or presentation. Whatever you choose to do, you must make sure that the lessons you plan provide children with the knowledge, models, and scaffolds they need to be successful with the final task. For example, if you expect children to create a written response to the question, it is a good idea to write a model answer before teaching the unit, which could be shared with children as an example. As a subject leader, you may wish to support teachers with this.

Historical enquiries and the wider curriculum

Finally, when planning for historical enquiries, it is best practice to consider how each question fits in with the wider history curriculum. This means that rather than planning each historical enquiry as a separate block of content, look at how your enquiries work together to build pupils understanding of the discipline over time. When you look at your curriculum as a whole, you can consider the breadth of the questions you set to ensure that you are asking a good variety of questions and not overly focusing on certain types of questions. You can also consider how pupils develop depth of understanding by applying what they have learned through tackling questions of each kind to build their substantive and disciplinary knowledge over time.

Case study: planning and teaching historical enquiries

Stephanie has been a history subject leader at her school for three years. In her first year of leadership, she attends training on historical enquiries through the Historical Association and, as a result, begins to incorporate this into her own practice. Seeing the success that she was having with her own class, in her second year of leadership, Stephanie asks all class teachers in her school to plan and teach a historical enquiry for each of their history topics. She is allocated one staff meeting to train teachers on how they should do this. However, a year on, Stephanie notices that some of the teachers are planning questions that are not historically framed, such as 'Would you rather be an Anglo-Saxon or a Viking?' and that across the curriculum, some disciplinary concepts are rarely looked at while others are covered multiple times. Stephanie concludes that they needed to look at their enquiry questions as a whole school rather than relying on each individual teacher to plan their own.

Stephanie leads the professional development session outlined below, and as a team, they agree the focus of each enquiry. Stephanie then maps this out for teachers:

	AUTUMN	SPRING	SUMMER
Year 1	**Sources and evidence:** What have archaeologists (and/or historians) learnt about the past from (insert an example, e.g. a local example like Must Farm)?	**Continuity and change:** To what extent has life in our local area changed since your grandparents were children?	**Historical significance:** Why do historians think Elizabeth I is a significant person to remember?
Year 2	**Sources and evidence:** What can we learn about (insert your town/village) in X (insert time period of study) from what has been left behind?	**Similarity and difference:** What was life like for people living in Tudor England?	**Historical significance, Consequence:** Why is Rosa Parks still remembered today?

	AUTUMN	SPRING	SUMMER
Year 3	**Continuity and change:** To what extent did life change in Britain from the Stone Age to the Iron Age?	**Sources and evidence:** What can we learn about Tutankhamun from what was found in his tomb?	**Similarity and difference:** To what extent were the experiences of people living in ancient Greece the same?
Year 4	**Causation:** What led to the fall of the Western Empire?	**Continuity and change:** To what extent did life change in England between 450 and 1066?	**Historical significance:** Why do historians study the Stuarts?
Year 5	**Sources and evidence:** What do these sources tell us about Baghdad at this time (900CE–1258)?	**Continuity and change, Similarity and difference:** To what extent did the Industrial Revolution change the lives of all people in Britain in the eighteenth century?	**Historical significance, Consequence:** How and why is the Victorian era remembered as being an 'age of innovation and progress'?
Year 6	**Similarity and difference:** To what extent were all women in Britain fighting for women's suffrage between 1830–1928?	**Causation:** What led to the Bristol bus boycotts?	**Consequence:** What impact did WWI have on Britain between 1918 and 1939?

While Stephanie is aware that they may wish to amend this plan over time as questions can always be improved, by having their historical enquiries mapped out in this way, she feels more confident that the curriculum is broad and balanced, and teachers feel better supported to teach historical enquiries effectively.

Teaching historical enquiry

When engaging in historical enquiries, you can make sure all pupils are successful by incorporating the following:

- explicit teaching
- prior knowledge retrieval
- lots of practice!

While these strategies are useful across the curriculum, we will look at these specifically through the lens of teaching history.

1. Explicit teaching

As mentioned at the start of this chapter, historical enquiry does not mean that children have to discover knowledge for themselves. Primary-aged pupils should not be expected to act like 'mini-historians', setting their own questions and conducting their own enquiries. Children do not have expert knowledge or access to the archives that academic historians have, so our history lessons need to include explicit teaching of new knowledge. Our teacher-led explanations must be clear and concise and break down new content into small, manageable steps (Rosenshine, 2012). To do this, you need to be clear about what you plan to teach children and think about how this could be broken down logically to avoid overloading children by presenting too much information all at once. For example, if you were looking at the causes of a particular event, you could take time to discuss each potential cause in depth before moving on to analysing the connections between them.

As part of your explicit teaching, you should provide models to the children (Rosenshine, 2012). This could include modelled paragraphs or essays that can be discussed with the children and/or through narrating the thought process that they need to go through when answering the question. For example, time could be spent unpicking what the question is asking and modelling how to apply your knowledge to structure a response.

While lessons should be teacher-led, this does not mean the teacher should be the only one talking in the classroom. As part of explicit teaching, the teacher needs to provide lots of opportunities for children to discuss what they are learning, routinely asking questions, checking for understanding, and then addressing any errors and/or misconceptions that arise. At the end of each lesson, the teacher can guide pupils to identify what they have learned from today's lesson that will support them with answering the enquiry question.

2. Prior knowledge retrieval

Retrieval practice is a teaching strategy that involves actively recalling previously taught content from memory in order to improve learning and recall. In the past few years, many teachers have incorporated 'retrieval practice' in their lessons in various ways, including through the use of regular quizzing. Evidence from cognitive science has taught us that retrieval practice can be a useful strategy because it helps to:

- **enhance memory recall** – engaging in regular retrieval practice can make recalling information quicker and easier (Karpicke, Lehman and Aue, 2014).

- **make connections and apply knowledge** – when retrieving prior knowledge becomes effortless, it no longer puts a strain on working memory, and therefore pupils find it easier to apply their knowledge in new contexts (Didau and Rose, 2016).

- **learn new things** – research shows that when we have some prior knowledge of a topic, we find it easier to learn more about it (Witherby and Carpenter, 2022).

- **check for understanding** – through retrieval practice, teachers can identify gaps in knowledge and check for errors and misconceptions (Fletcher-Wood, 2018).

There are three main types of retrieval you may choose to use in the classroom:

1. **Recognition tests** – for example, multiple-choice quizzing or true/false questions. This type of retrieval requires children to select the correct response from a selection of possible answers.

2. **Cued recall** – for example, providing children with an image to label or a photograph or diagram to help them answer a question. This type of retrieval is usually more difficult than a recognition test as the child needs to recall the information from memory using the cue to support them rather than identifying the correct answer.

3. **Free recall** – for example, asking a question without providing any clues to help pupils remember. This type of retrieval is often the most challenging as it requires children to recall information without any support.

Given the identified benefits of routine retrieval practice, it is unsurprising that many schools have sought to embed this practice across the curriculum. However, you must be careful when applying generic approaches across disciplines to ensure you do not lose connection with the substance of the subject. Just because you could start every lesson with five 'do now' multiple-choice questions does not mean that you should! You need to think about how you can utilise the benefits of this practice in a way that respects the uniqueness of the discipline. In history, you can do this by:

- using quizzing, including multiple-choice quizzes, to recall knowledge that you want children to have at their 'fingertips' when they are writing so that they can focus on their argument rather than overloading their working memory trying to remember specific facts.

- utilising the benefits of retrieval when storytelling by asking pupils to retrieve prior knowledge at parts of the narrative where children will benefit from making connections with previously learned content (Counsell, 2023).

- activating prior knowledge that is relevant to new learning at the start of a lesson. For example, before starting a lesson on democracy in the twentieth century, ask children to recall what they already know about 'democracy' from what they have studied before.

- using timelines to retrieve and order prior knowledge.

While retrieval practice can be highly effective in history, you must always be clear about its purpose when you are using it. It can be effective to quiz pupils on relevant factual information (such as key dates) during a topic so that pupils have this knowledge at their 'fingertips' when they come to write a response to an enquiry question. However, providing a decontextualised quiz at the end of the year to check children still remember every key date they have ever been taught is not an effective use of time.

3. Practice

Practice is needed to get better at anything. Just as children need to have lots of practice throwing and catching in PE, they need to have practice answering enquiry questions in history. This includes plenty of scaffolded and guided practice to ensure high levels of success before moving on to independent practice (Archer and Hughes, 2011).

In practice: scaffolding to support with enquiry

There are a number of ways you can provide scaffolding to support children with historical enquiry.

Examples of scaffolds: sentence stems

'One similarity between X and Y is…'

'One difference is…'

'X is a historically significant person because…'

'One reason why X is still remembered today is…'

'Some historians have argued that…'

'One significant change that occurred during this period was…'

Examples of scaffolds: word banks

The Stone Age to the Iron Age		
archaeologist	tomb	Stone Age
artefact	crop	Palaeolithic
Prehistory	farm	Mesolithic
excavation	agriculture	Neolithic
Beaker	quern stone	Bronze Age
migration	fort	Iron Age
hunter-gatherer	Druid	hillforts
nomad	conflict	long barrow
trade	loom	wattle and daub

Examples of scaffolds: knowledge organisers

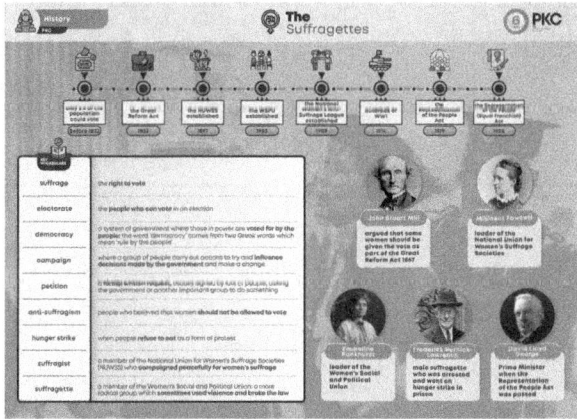

Figure 5.1: an example of a knowledge organiser about the Suffragettes

Examples of scaffolds: writing frames and structure strips

To what extent were all women in Britain fighting for women's suffrage between 1830–1928?
Introduction What is suffrage? What was democracy like in early nineteenth century? Outline the argument you plan to make to answer the question
Section 1: Suffragists (NUWSS) What did they do? Who were they? Who were they were fighting for?
Section 2: Suffragettes (WSPU) What did they do? Who were they? Who were they were fighting for?
Section 3: Anti-suffrage Who were they? What did they believe? What were they fighting for?
Conclusion Summarise your answer to the question – were ALL women fighting for women's suffrage? Did all men and women think the same and want the same thing?
Key people and dates: **1832:** Great Reform Act **1867**: Second Reform Act (John Stuart Mill) **1897**: The National Union of Women's Suffrage Societies (NUWSS) (Millicent Fawcett) **1903**: Women's Social and Political Union (WSPU) (Emmeline Pankhurst) **1908**: the Women's National Anti-Suffrage League **1910:** the National League for Opposing Women's Suffrage **1918**: the Representation of the People Act **1928**: all women able to vote

Figure 5.2: an example of a structure strip about women's suffrage

While scaffolding and guided practice are important, this type of support can be reduced gradually in lessons as children's knowledge and skills develop (Pearce, 2022). One strategy you might use to gradually fade support is, 'I do, we do, you do' where you model the task to the class first (e.g. writing a paragraph to answer an enquiry question), then you have a go at writing one as a class or in pairs/groups (we do), before asking children to write independently (you do). Independent practice is important, so make sure that over time children have more and more opportunities to apply their growing knowledge to answer their enquiry questions.

Chapter summary

- A 'historical enquiry' is a series of lessons that are connected by a focus on answering a historically-framed 'enquiry question.'
- Enquiry questions need to be precise and 'historically valid'. This means that the question needs to be framed through the lens of one (or possibly two) disciplinary concepts.
- Disciplinary concepts in history relate to cause, consequence, continuity and change, similarity and difference, historical significance, sources and evidence, and interpretation.
- Historical enquiries need to be planned to guide children through the enquiry process, sequencing knowledge across a series of lessons to enable them to answer the question at the end.
- We should teach historical enquiries explicitly, encouraging children to retrieve and build on prior knowledge and ensuring they have opportunities for guided and independent practice.

Questions for reflection

- What is a historical enquiry, and why is it important?
- How do we use historical enquiry in our school?
- To what extent are the enquiry questions we use precise and historically framed?
- How is historical enquiry planned and taught in our school, and is there anything I would like to do to improve this?

Example PD session: historical enquiry

Here is an example of what a PD session on historical enquiry could look like.

TIMING SUGGESTION	SESSION GUIDANCE
5 mins	Recap from the last staff training session on substantive and disciplinary knowledge. Do a short quiz on disciplinary and substantive concepts and discuss responses as a team.
5 mins	Highlight the importance of historical enquiry in primary history, using this chapter and the suggested reading in 'Explore further'.
15 mins	Explain what makes a good enquiry question, showing examples and non-examples. Provide teachers with the checklist in this chapter for writing good enquiry questions and ask them to look at a series of questions and discuss how effective they are.
20 mins	Provide teachers with your curriculum map and ask them to look at what they currently teach and think about how they could plan for effective historical enquiry, (if they are already doing this, look at how it could be improved). Spend the rest of the session collaboratively planning for historical enquiry and end the session sharing the next steps.

Explore further

- Michael Riley's (2008) article, 'Into the Key Stage 3 history garden: choosing and planting your enquiry questions', found in *Teaching History* volume 99

- The Historical Association's (2020) article, 'What's the wisdom on enquiry questions?', found in *Teaching History* volume 178

- Barak Rosenshine's (2012) article, 'Principles of instruction: Research-based strategies that all teachers should know', found in *American Educator* volume 36

6 Narratives and storytelling

In this chapter, we will explore the importance of narrative in history. A narrative in history is a story being presented about events in the past. As a history subject leader, it is important to understand that telling stories is more than just an effective pedagogical device, but it is also 'the way meaning is made and it is the very object of study' in history (Counsell, 2023). The history of humanity is made up of a wealth of rich and diverse stories. These stories help us to make sense of what came before by introducing us to the people, the places and the experiences that have shaped the world we live in today. Through studying our history, we seek to construct and make sense of these stories, understand how they relate to each other, and ultimately challenge them, to gain a deeper understanding of our past.

In this chapter, we will:

- explore the importance of narrative in history.
- look at the evidence base that highlights the 'privileged status of story', and how you can best utilise storytelling as a pedagogical device.
- identify practical ways you can embed storytelling in your classroom.
- look at how narratives can be woven through the history curriculum to build chronological understanding and support children with both making and challenging generalisations.
- discuss the importance of including diverse stories to ensure a more equitable and accurate account of the past.

Narrative in history

Counsell argues that narrative is history's 'chief mode of accounting' (Counsell, 2023). This means constructing narratives is the main way historians make meaning in history. The events of the past are not merely facts to be revived by historians. Past events become 'history' when they are transformed into a narrative in order to be explained (Munslow, 2018). Historians make important choices when they narrate these stories, deciding what to include or discount to construct their own account of the past.

As a subject leader, you need to consider how to support teachers and children with recognising the importance of narrative, as this is fundamental to understanding the discipline of history. One way you can do this is to ensure that you do not teach history as 'the past'. The 'past' and 'history' are different. The 'past' is everything that happened or existed before now. Whereas, as discussed in Chapter 1, 'history' is concerned with the narratives produced by historians to make meaning of the past (Munslow, 2018). To simplify this for primary children, you can describe history not as 'the past' or '*the* story of the past' but instead as 'the stories people tell about the past.'

Through your history lessons, you should emphasise the importance of narrative by telling stories of the past and supporting children with making meaning from them. Effective teaching in history is not disseminating long lists of facts to be memorised. In history, we are storytellers. A history lesson without storytelling is like a PE lesson with no movement, or a music lesson with no sound. Not only are narratives fundamental to the discipline, but you should not underestimate the power of stories in captivating children's interests and making the past feel relevant.

The privileged status of story

Interestingly, humans have used storytelling as a means of transmitting knowledge for thousands of years. Research from the last 30 years has shown us why. According to psychologists, stories are 'psychologically privileged', meaning that they are processed differently from other types of materials (Willingham, 2002). According to Willingham, there appears to be something inherent in the story format that makes stories more interesting, easier to understand and more likely to be remembered. This is because the familiar nature of the format of stories makes them easier to comprehend than other forms of text (Graesser et al., 1994) and the causal connections made through stories create a web of cues that mean that if we can recall one part of the story, we are likely to remember another.

Mar et al. have provided further evidence to support the claim that stories are easier to understand and remember. They conducted a meta-analysis of experiments that looked at memory and/or comprehension of narrative versus expository texts. Their research concluded that people find it easier to understand and remember information presented in a story compared with the information presented in an essay (Mar et al., 2021). Therefore, as subject leaders, it is clear that utilising the power of stories is an effective tool for teaching, as children are more likely to understand and remember what we teach them if we present it to them in this format.

While there is no universal agreement on what makes a story a story, Willingham explains that there are general principles that can be applied. These are sometimes referred to as the 'Four Cs'. He argues that history is a natural story as it has the four Cs – causality, conflicts, complications, and character – built in (Willingham, 2002).

- **Causality** refers to how events are causally related to one another. As discussed in Chapter 3, the concept of 'causation' is an important one for historians.

- **Conflicts** arise in stories, usually as a central character has obstacles to face that make it difficult for them to reach their goal.

- Stories are made more exciting through additional **complications,** or 'subproblems', that appear and give the story more depth.

- Finally, a good story has to have strong, interesting **characters**.

An example of how we can apply the four C's: Boudicca

Character:
A strong, interesting character: Boudicca

Causality: Boudicca fought the Romans as they mistreated her and her daughters and took their land

A very long time ago, a warrior queen named Boudicca led the Iceni tribe in the south-east of England. At this time, parts of Britain had been invaded by the Roman Empire. Boudicca had inherited land when her husband died. However, the Romans took her land away from her, and treated her and her daughters very cruelly. Boudicca decided to fight back!

While most of the Roman army was away fighting in North Wales, Boudicca led her army to St Albans, Colchester, and London, where she destroyed the towns and killed thousands of people. However, when the Roman army returned, Boudicca was faced with a disciplined, well-trained, and better-equipped opponent. Her army was eventually defeated at the Battle of Watling Street.

While Boudicca's rebellion was unsuccessful, she is remembered today as a symbol of freedom and courage.

Conflict: our protagonist, Boudicca, wants to be able to own her own land and rule the Iceni Tribe but is being prevented to do so by the invading Roman army

Complications: after successfully attacking St Albans, Colchester and London, Boudicca's rebel army faced the well trained, better equipped Roman army

Figure 6.1: An example of applying the four C's to Boudicca

Storytelling as a pedagogical device

Stories can be presented to children in history as written narratives or through oral storytelling. Free, online versions of historical stories can be accessed through websites such as BBC Bitesize and the National Geographic. Some teachers have even started using AI as a starting point for constructing stories, although this should be used cautiously and checked for accuracy. Many teachers use oral storytelling in history without realising they are doing it, as the nature of the discipline means it is difficult to teach without engaging with narratives. Whether you are teaching about the invasion and settlement of Anglo-Saxons or the rise of early Islamic civilisation, presenting children with the knowledge of what happened through a story format rather than as a list of facts is more memorable and engaging. For example:

LIST OF FACTS	STORY FORMAT
• Howard Carter was an archaeologist and Egyptologist. • Howard Carter and his team discovered the tomb of Tutankhamun on 26th November, 1922. • Tutankhamun died around 3000 years ago. • It is believed Tutankhamun became Pharaoh when he was around nine years old. • Tutankhamun reigned for approximately ten years before passing away around 18 or 19 years old. • The tomb contained 5,398 items including a golden death mask, trumpets, a dagger and fresh linen.	Over one hundred years ago, there lived an archaeologist called Howard Carter, who was fascinated with ancient Egypt. In 1922, Carter and his team would make a discovery that would captivate the world. On the 26th November 1922, Carter entered a room that had remained sealed for over 3000 years and discovered the tomb of Tutankhamun. In the words of Carter, the tomb contained a 'strange and wonderful medley of extraordinary and beautiful objects', including a golden death mask, trumpets, a dagger and fresh linen. All 5,398 objects once belonged to the 'boy king' Tutankhamun, who after inheriting the throne when he was around nine years old, reigned for roughly ten years before passing away.

When planning lessons in history, you may wish to source pre-written stories online, through schemes or texts or create them yourself. If you create them yourself, you can prepare by listing the main parts of the story and key vocabulary to aid memory. The benefit of writing and telling your own versions of historical stories is that you can make sure the language you use is both age-appropriate and challenging and ensure that your stories contain the historical knowledge you want your pupils to learn.

When using storytelling as a way of teaching new content in history, it is important that pupils are actively engaged, thinking deeply about the story, and participating in the lesson. You can use questioning to check for understanding, ensuring that children fully comprehend important aspects of the story such as: who was involved and why, what happened, how did it happen, why might it have happened, what was the impact of what happened, and how do we know? You may also check understanding by asking pupils to retell the story, individually or in pairs or groups, with as much detail as possible. This could be done verbally or as part of written work, and take place during the lesson, or later on in the sequence of learning.

Historical imagination

The stories we tell in history provide a window into another world. Hill argues that the past is often a remote, strange and unfamiliar place to our pupils. Therefore, when teaching history, we should borrow the techniques used by authors of fictional literature and engage in 'world building' to support children with understanding what the past might have looked like (Hill, 2020). The historian, Staley, has argued that using our imagination is key in history. According to Staley, as historians have to draw inferences from often fragmented and partial evidential records, they need to use their imagination to help them fill in the gaps (Staley, 2020). Enabling pupils to imagine the past supports them with an understanding of history. When engrossed in a story, we imagine ourselves in new places, enduring new experiences and experiencing real emotions that bring us closer to understanding what life was like for people who lived before us.

However, while you may encourage pupils to use their imaginations in history lessons, you must make sure that the stories you tell them are rooted in evidence and avoid making up or adding in unnecessary details that could lead to misconceptions. For example, in the story above, it would be inappropriate to try to sensationalise the narrative by talking about curses that may have been bestowed on all who entered the tomb of the mummy When storytelling, you should be aware of the 'seductive details effect'. Seductive details are interesting pieces of information that are irrelevant to learning. Research has shown that pupils exposed to seductive details learn less than those who are not (Sundararajan and Adesope, 2020).

While a historian is unavoidably intertwined with the history they produce (Munslow, 2018), you must remember that the characters in your historical narratives do not belong to you as they would in a fictional novel. While we will always be influenced to an extent by our worldviews, we need to be aware of how our own perspectives can influence our pupils. One way you can do this is to think carefully about the language you use in history lessons, and try to avoid dramatising characters or ascribing them as 'goodies' or 'baddies' like we might find in a fictional story.

In practice: using language carefully

Instead of saying: *King John was the worst king in history! He was a cruel tyrant, and everyone hated him.*

We could say: *King John was one of the most controversial kings in history. Following his death, he has often been portrayed as a cruel tyrant.*

When did the story take place?

When storytelling in history, you also need to consider the language used to describe when the story took place – how long ago – and the passing of time. You need to be aware of the mathematical knowledge underpinning an understanding of chronology and ensure the language used is age-appropriate. Just because younger children do not have the mathematical knowledge to understand the numbers or scale of time passing, it does not mean that they should not have access to the rich stories of the past. Instead, you can use phrases such as 'a long time ago, when your grandparents were still little' to help them understand that this happened in the past.

Using images and maps

Another way you can help pupils understand and remember historical stories is through the use of images and maps. Dual coding theory suggests that combining images alongside verbal and written information can increase the chances of information being learned and understood. According to 'dual coding theory', we process verbal and visual information through separate channels, so when we are provided with information in these two formats, it gives us two ways of remembering information later on (Pavio, 1986). Therefore, dual coding can enhance learning. However, you must ensure that the images are relevant and useful and be aware that sometimes combining too many words and visuals can lead to cognitive overload, which can harm learning (Sweller and Chandler, 1994). For example, displaying pictures of different trees when discussing the concept of a family tree would not enhance learning as these images would not support the children with understanding this concept and could become distracting instead.

Examples of useful images to use in history lessons are:

Paintings of the people being studied	 **Figure 6.2:** *Portrait of Elizabeth I*	Teachers could use paintings to show children what people in the past might have looked like. Portraits can also be studied as important historical sources.
Photographs of artefacts	 **Figure 6.3:** *Death mask of Tutankhamun*	Photographs of real artefacts are fascinating and show the children first-hand how we can find out about the past through the objects left behind. For example, the death mask of Tutankhamun could be shown when studying the Ancient Egyptians. Not only is this artefact an incredible work of art, we can also learn lots about Egyptian beliefs around death and the afterlife through studying it.

Maps of places in the past	**Figure 6.4:** *An old map of Westminster and Southwark*	Maps can be used to provide locational knowledge, as well as important topographical information, such as the layout of the land, access to a river etc. Maps from the past can also be used to compare with the present day.
Paintings or photographs	**Figure 6.5:** *Photograph of a school classroom*	Photographs or paintings can be used to depict what life might have looked like at the time. For example, this photograph shows inside a school classroom. Images like this could be used to give children a deeper understanding of what life was like during the time period being studied.
Symbols	**Figure 6.6:** *Crown symbol*	Symbols can be used to depict key concepts and vocabulary being taught, such as the symbol of a crown for 'monarchy'. As a school, we may agree to use consistent symbols when discussing key concepts to aid memory. For example, using this symbol of a crown each time the children learn about the monarchy will help them to remember that a monarch is a king or queen.

Historical fiction

Narratives in history differ from historical fiction as historians seek to know the truth and attempt to present the story as accurately to the past as the evidence will allow. While historical fiction aims to evoke the spirit of a particular historical period, authors take creative liberties to craft a compelling and immersive story that resonates with readers. Despite this, there are benefits to reading carefully selected historical fiction in school. Tiffany argues that fictional texts can 'add richness and valuable hinterland knowledge in a purposeful and engaging way'

(Tiffany, 2023). However, both Lang (2003) and Levstik (1995) have argued that children will often accept stories presented to them uncritically and therefore require guidance from teachers to differentiate between fact and fiction. For example, reading *The Prince and the Pauper* could support children in imagining what life in Tudor England may have looked like for both the rich and the poor. However, when sharing this text, you would need to make it clear that historical evidence does not support the narrative that Prince Edward Tudor temporarily swapped lives with a pauper who looked identical to him.

Weaving narratives and scale-switching

Over time, the stories you tell through the curriculum support children with developing chronological knowledge. Chronological knowledge is about more than ordering events on a timeline and memorising key dates, it is also understanding the broader features of particular historical periods. This is often referred to as developing a 'sense of period'. One way you can support pupils to do this is through telling the 'big stories' of the past. These overarching narratives can be fleshed out with smaller-scale stories to add richness and complexity. The act of changing the scale of the period being studied, from broader overviews to smaller-scale stories, is known as 'scale-switching'. According to Michael Fordham, switching the scale between the macro and the micro means our pupils can benefit from spaced retrieval of historical knowledge (Fordham, 2014). This is because children must retrieve prior knowledge to apply the broader overviews to the smaller-scale stories being studied, or vice versa.

Weaving rich narratives on different scales through the curriculum can also teach children about how historians question established narratives. For example, when teaching children about the Neolithic Revolution in Britain, you could start by telling them the story of how the introduction of farming led to the wide-scale transition from a hunter-gatherer lifestyle to one of agriculture. This meant that people no longer had to live nomadic lives and were able to settle in one place. You could then challenge this narrative and tell the story of the discovery of the Mesolithic Howick House in Northumberland, which appears to dispute the idea that all people at this time were nomadic. Introducing pupils to stories in this way encourages them to question narratives and provides a meaningful context to invite children to join in with historical debates.

Local stories

Another way you can meaningfully incorporate both the 'macro' and the 'micro' in the history curriculum is to study how local small-scale stories, or 'microhistories', illustrate national and global trends and developments. For example, you could look at the impact of the Industrial Revolution both nationally and in your local area. Rich local stories can show children how their local area has been shaped over time by those who lived before them, and how their community has contributed to the history of Britain and the wider world. It is important to support pupils with making these connections, rather than viewing a 'local study' in isolation. If you focus your curriculum content around interesting local heroes and fascinating stories without an understanding of the wider overview of the period, the stories you tell through the curriculum risk becoming disconnected and easily forgotten. As Guyver warns, a 'multiplicity of microhistories may neglect some bigger events, further afield, of significance, which affect the local picture' (Guyver, 2000).

Therefore, in order to support pupils with developing chronological knowledge, including a secure 'sense of period', it is important to provide pupils with both the 'bigger stories' which outline the broader aspects of the period across a wider timescale and space, as well as studying in depth the smaller-scale stories which add detail and richness, including local stories where appropriate.

In practice: scale-switching

Here are two examples of teachers using 'scale-switching' to support their pupils to understand the past.

KS1 example:

Rosa Parks

Gemma is teaching about the 'significant individual' Rosa Parks to Year 2. She has identified that Rosa Parks' story is a smaller-scale story that fits in with the 'bigger narrative' of the Civil Rights Movement in the USA.

Lessons 1–2

Gemma decides that it would be good to start by setting the scene before learning about Rosa Parks. She identifies that the children need to understand that the story took place in America, a long time ago when their grandparents were either very young, or possibly not even born yet. Gemma decides that to support children in developing their chronological understanding, she will look at this time frame in relation to other things they have studied in history, e.g. this happened before King Charles II was crowned and a long time after the Great Fire of the London.

The children need to know that at the time there were 'segregation laws' – these were rules that said that Black Americans and White Americans had to go to different schools and were not allowed to sit together on public transport. At this time, Black Americans were often treated badly and some people were trying to stop this unfair treatment.

Lessons 3–4

Gemma decides that once the children understand the bigger picture, they will learn all about Rosa Parks, including what she did (refused to give up her seat to a White person on the bus) and what happened as a result (the Montgomery Bus Boycott).

Lessons 5–6

Once the children understand what Rosa Parks did, Gemma decides she would like to challenge them further by discussing the impact that Rosa Parks had on the wider Civil Rights Movement and why she is still remembered today.

KS2 example:

The Industrial Revolution

Amir is teaching his Year 5 class about the Industrial Revolution in Britain. He has identified that he wants to look at the bigger picture in relation to the Industrial Revolution in Britain and its impact abroad, as well as providing rich, 'small scale stories' that tell the story through the eyes of people in the local area.

Lesson 1

Amir decides it would be useful to begin the unit by retrieving prior learning that can be built upon. For example, Amir knows that the children have learned about 'urban' and 'rural' areas, 'trade' and 'migration' in geography, so he asks them to recall and discuss what these terms mean. He explains to the children that across human history there have been significant turning points that have drastically transformed the way people think and act, making huge changes to how people live their lives. He provides an example of this which the children have already learned about – the 'agricultural revolution' – and explains that the 'Industrial Revolution' was another revolution like this.

Amir uses his first two lessons to set the scene, focusing on what life was like before and during this period. He asks the children to close their eyes as he provides them with a rich description of life before and during the Industrial Revolution. He focuses the lesson on answering the question: what changed and what stayed the same? As the children in Amir's class have some prior knowledge of the British Empire, he supports them by making the connection between the cotton being grown by enslaved African people in plantations and the cotton being spun by workers in British factories. By doing this, he increases the scale of the study, showing children the wider international impact of the Industrial Revolution in Britain.

Lessons 2–5

Once the children understand what the Industrial Revolution was, Amir moves on to focus on some of the key developments that took place at the time. He decides he would like to focus in more depth on the growth of factories, including the use of child labour, as this will allow him to incorporate some interesting local stories. He also focuses on the invention of the steam engine and the growth of the railways. Again, looking closely through the local lens. Amir spends a lesson looking in depth at Richard Arkwright's story, including his spinning frame and the first factories, before moving on to look at a local factory. He plans a trip to visit the site to further support pupils in imagining what life was like at the time. He then moves on to look at the invention of the steam engine and the railways, focusing on the first railway in their local town, utilising local historical sources, such as photographs and old maps, to help bring the stories to life.

After studying those smaller-scale local histories, Amir decides to switch the scale back again to the wider narrative. Now that the children have a lot of knowledge about the Industrial Revolution, he supports them by focusing on the similarities and differences between the lives of people at the time. He wants children to make the distinction between what life was like for the people who owned the factories, in comparison to those that worked inside them. As a class, they spend time discussing both the similarities and differences, evaluating how similar life was, along with how different life was, before recording their arguments in an essay, using local and national examples to illustrate their points.

Diverse stories

Through the history curriculum, schools have the power to decide which stories are told. For every story chosen, millions more remain untold. Schools have a great deal of autonomy over what stories are shared and not shared with pupils. This freedom comes with great responsibility. With endless possibilities, you can find yourself faced with the dilemma of there being so many powerful stories to tell in so little time.

One way to decide what stories should 'make the cut' in your curriculum is to consider *breadth* and *balance*. It is important that the curriculum includes stories across a wide range of times and places, including different groups of people and different experiences.

It is important to show multiple perspectives, ensuring you are not always telling a single version of a story. Through hearing stories through many different voices, across time and place, pupils can begin to understand the complexity of perspective. One way of incorporating multiple perspectives into stories is to tell them from two different perspectives, for example, from the perspective of a rich person and a poor person, or a man and a woman. This can work well in helping children make generalisations about what life was like for different groups of people.

In the 'Research Review Series: History', Ofsted argue that 'generalisations are powerful tools of historical description, but pupils must also explore their limitations in capturing the complexity and diversity of past societies or lived experiences' (Ofsted, 2021). This means that over time, you can begin to 'capture the complexity' of these stories by showing how the lived experiences of particular groups of people were not all the same.

For example, if pupils learn about the Suffragette movement, they could learn that not all women had the same experiences at the time. In fact, it is important that pupils understand that this campaign was not fought by women against men. Those campaigning for women's suffrage were not one homogenous group. While they may have had some similar experiences and ideals, they included both men (for example, Frederick Pethick-Lawrence) and women of different ethnicities (for example, Sophia Duleep Singh), they came from very different backgrounds and were, at times, campaigning for different things. For example, some suffragists were campaigning for women to have equal voting rights to men at the time, which would have excluded many women. There were also huge disagreements within the movement about the tactics being used, such as the use of violence. Millicent Fawcett who led the 'Suffragist' movement, campaigned through the use of petitions and non-violent marches, whereas Emmeline Pankhurst, who led the 'Suffragettes', deployed more militant tactics, such as smashing windows, planting bombs and setting fire to public buildings. Similarly, those opposing the suffrage movement were also not a homogenous group. It can surprise children to learn that many women were actively opposing their own right to vote. Even the most powerful woman at the time, Queen Victoria, in 1870 described the suffrage movement as a 'mad, wicked folly'.

Telling stories like this through a diversity of voices enables pupils to analyse similarities and differences between people, groups and experiences during a period or event, gradually allowing them to challenge generalisations and develop a more nuanced understanding of the past. Therefore, providing children with a wide range of diverse stories not only ensures a more equitable view of history, but also a more accurate one.

Chapter summary

- A narrative in history is a story being presented about events in the past.
- Research has shown that telling stories is an effective way of teaching new content in history.
- You can tell stories using written texts, including historical fiction, as well as oral storytelling.

- You can develop pupils' chronological knowledge, including a growing 'sense of period', by providing them with both the 'big stories' that outline the broader features of the period and 'small scale' stories that add richness and detail.

- It is important that schools consider breadth and balance when deciding what stories to tell through the curriculum and aim to show multiple perspectives where possible.

Questions for reflection

- What stories do we teach in history and why?
- How do the stories we teach support children with developing their chronological knowledge, including a growing 'sense of period'?
- How and where can we use storytelling to teach new content in history?

Example PD session: narrative in history

Here is an example of what a PD session on narrative in history could look like:

TIMING SUGGESTION	SESSION GUIDANCE
5 mins	Highlight the importance of narrative in history, using the section on 'Narrative in history' above.
10 mins	Share Willingham's article on 'The Privileged Status of Story' and ask teachers why they think telling stories is important in history.
15 mins	Using the examples (e.g. the Ancient Egyptian 'list vs. story format' and/or the 4C's Boudicca story) model to teachers how they could incorporate storytelling in history lessons.
20 mins	Provide teachers with the opportunity to look at their next history topic and begin planning the stories they wish to teach. If there is time, teachers could have a go at sharing these stories with a partner or as a group.

Explore further

- Michael Hill's (2020) article, 'Curating the imagined past: world building in the history curriculum', in *Teaching History*, volume 180
- Daniel T Willingham's (2002) article 'The Privileged Status of Story', available on The American Federation of Teachers website here: https://www.aft.org/ae/summer2004/willingham

7 Disciplinary literacy

In this chapter, we will focus on disciplinary literacy: what this looks like in history, and how we can improve how children speak, read and write in history lessons. As subject leaders, we should consider what is unique about our subject in terms of speaking, reading and writing. This chapter will help you understand the nuanced ways of communicating in history and how you can better support your pupils in applying their literacy skills in purposeful and meaningful ways in their history lessons.

In this chapter, we will:

- learn what disciplinary literacy is and why it is important in history.
- identify the subject-specific ways that historians speak, read, and write.
- look at the importance of building vocabulary in history.
- consider how you can embed disciplinary literacy in your school, using practical examples and case studies to help you.

What is disciplinary literacy?

Disciplinary literacy refers to how we think, speak, read, and write in each subject. Each academic discipline has its unique way of creating, communicating and evaluating knowledge, which often goes untaught or is misunderstood (Mortimore, 2020). Mortimore argues that while many schools adopt whole-school literacy initiatives across the curriculum, they often struggle to marry up generalised approaches with the subtle – but highly specific – ways we communicate within each discipline. Therefore, disciplinary literacy can provide us with the crucial bridge between embedding general literacy practices across our curriculum and explicitly teaching subject-specific ways of speaking, reading, and writing.

Speaking like a historian

In England, the National Curriculum clearly states that we must teach pupils to talk and listen. Recently, there have been calls for 'oracy' to be more prominent in our classrooms. The term oracy was first coined by Andrew Wilkinson in 1965 (Wilkinson, 1965). In his paper, he was clear that oracy was not a subject that should be taught discretely. Instead, he argues that we should teach children to speak and listen through the academic subjects we already teach.

Speaking and listening are important for many reasons. Firstly, talking and thinking are intimately intertwined. Language competence underpins cognitive development (Sealy, 2024). Engaging in purposeful talk helps children to think hard about the new content that has been taught. In history, you can encourage children to apply their knowledge to discuss the arguments that historians have with each other. For example, you could explain that some historians argue about the causes of particular events and they provide evidence to justify their arguments. By engaging in discussions around causal arguments, children can meaningfully apply what they have learned in history.

You should aim to create a classroom culture where you listen to and value every child's voice. However, you need to be careful not to suggest that all opinions about history are equally valid. Sealy argues that if we teach pupils that we should value all opinions equally without understanding the role of knowledge in forming opinions and the importance of evidence, then we are stepping into 'dangerous territory' (Sealy, 2024). Therefore, it is important to emphasise to children that their arguments must be convincing in a subject like history, where there can be many interpretations. To do this, you have to apply your knowledge to provide 'evidence' to justify your argument. As a subject leader, you must remember that children need to have a secure knowledge base to engage in purposeful discussions. They have to have something to talk about and understand that historical claims require 'evidence'.

Vocabulary

To understand a subject, you need to understand its language (Quigley, 2018). Therefore, a way to set your pupils up for success is to explicitly teach them the language of history. Words are powerful tools in history for developing precise and nuanced thinking, understanding and communicating effectively (Woodcock, 2005). Woodcock argues that developing pupils' vocabularies and expertise in using and applying words makes them better historians. This is because words are not simply tools for speaking and writing but are 'tools of thought' that we need to imagine, speculate, and organise our ideas. For example, if you introduce pupils to the words that historians might use to describe change, such as 'shift', 'turning point', 'adjustment', 'evolution', 'reform', or 'revolution', pupils can think more deeply about the type or nature of change.

Teaching vocabulary effectively is about much more than memorising definitions for key words. Children need to develop rich background knowledge to understand new words in different contexts. For example, while pupils might be given a simple definition for the word 'trade', across the curriculum, they can add to their understanding of this concept through multiple encounters with 'trade' across time and place (e.g. trade in early Britain, Roman trade, trade and the British Empire). Vocabulary related to substantive concepts like 'trade' or 'democracy' (as discussed in Chapter 3) is likely to be highly generative, enabling pupils to learn more over time. Quigley describes these words as 'mental Velcro' (Quigley, 2018). As a subject leader, you may wish to consider which words you teach across the curriculum that will act like 'mental Velcro' for your pupils.

You can teach vocabulary in many ways. You may introduce children to key vocabulary at the start of the lesson and ask them to practise orally rehearsing new words so that they feel comfortable saying them out loud. When introducing new words, you could provide children with images to help them understand their meaning or put them in context within a sentence or story. Looking at the word's etymology can be a powerful way of teaching new vocabulary. Etymology is the study of the origin, or history, of the word. For example, if you were teaching children about the Stone Age in Britain, you could introduce them to the words Palaeolithic, Mesolithic, and Neolithic. These words were coined in 1865 by John Lubbock. He used the term 'lithic', from the Greek word for 'stone' (lithos). 'Palaeo' comes from the Greek 'palacios' meaning 'old', 'meso' is from the Greek 'mesos', meaning 'middle', and 'neo', meaning 'new'. Therefore, we can remember which period each word stands for by remembering:

- lithic = stone
- palaeo = old
- meso = middle
- neo = new

Reading like a historian

Reading in history lessons should be an essential element of teaching history. In primary school, it is common for children to read historical fiction as part of their history curriculum or as part of a wider topic. As discussed in Chapter 6, historical fiction can provide a great way in for primary pupils. Children need to have been taught vocabulary and background knowledge to infer meaning from what they read and understand the text. Reading historical fiction is a powerful way of igniting a love for history and developing a sense of period. However, you should be cautious about which texts you choose to include in your curriculum, as some texts can embed historical inaccuracies or portray problematic narratives. For example, *The Boy in the Striped Pyjamas* has been accused of perpetrating inaccuracies about the Holocaust (Randall, 2019). An age-appropriate alternative to reading this could be *When Hitler Stole Pink Rabbit* by Judith Kerr.

Some fictional texts written in the past can also be the object of study in our history lessons, as we can learn a lot about the language, beliefs, culture, and worldviews through the author's perspective. The Historical Association has a useful chronological historical fiction list with suggested fictional texts for all ages and periods. However, reading in history is about more than just reading historical fiction.

Reading in history could be part of a whole-school literacy initiative across the curriculum. While nothing is wrong with this, as a subject leader you need to be clear how reading in history differs from reading in other subjects, such as science or maths.

How is reading in history different from reading in other subjects?

Firstly, when we read in history, we place a significant emphasis on *who* wrote the text. In other words, we read with an eye on our author. This differs from how we might read in maths or science, where the author's background might be less important to us. Considering the author or source of the document when interpreting a text is known as 'sourcing' (Wineburg, 1998). We can do this by asking questions, such as:

- Who wrote this, or how did this source come about?
- Why was it written?
- What do we know about the author?

- To what extent was the author in a position to know about what they are writing about?
- What is the author's viewpoint or argument?

Historians also 'contextualise' the text by considering the circumstances that surround it. We can do this by considering questions such as:

- When was this source/text written?
- What was happening at the time?
- Who was the intended audience?

Furthermore, historians are expected to read multiple sources and 'corroborate' evidence. This means that when we read history, we need to make comparisons between texts before accepting any details as true. Only then can we piece the parts together from multiple sources to form a narrative or argument.

One aspect of reading in history that can be difficult for pupils is reading between the lines and looking for the subtext – the hidden meaning behind the text. You can remind pupils that when we read sources in history, we are rarely the intended audience. Reading sources in history is like eavesdropping in on someone else's conversation and we need to think about the motives of the person speaking and their intended audience. Therefore, rather than viewing sources as a means of gaining information or facts, we should view them as social exchanges where what is said is inseparable from who said it and in what context (Wineburg, 1991).

Teaching children to read like historians

You can teach children to read like historians by explicitly teaching them the distinctions between how historians read compared to how we might read in other subjects. You can teach 'sourcing', 'contextualising', and 'corroborating' by reading sources aloud to your pupils and modelling the thought processes that historians go through, using the questions above to guide you. You can also annotate sources with the children following an 'I do', 'we do' and 'you do' approach (as discussed in Chapter 5), asking pupils to highlight or underline key aspects of the text that you want to bring their attention to. You could also ask children to consider what further questions they have now that they have read the source. This will help them to understand that sources often provide historians with more questions than answers. You could also provide contrasting accounts or documents and ask children to consider how and why they differ.

As well as reading sources in history, we might ask them to read PowerPoint slides or booklets, magazines, timelines, textbooks, website text or blogs. Some primary schools have even tried introducing carefully chosen historical scholarship to pupils, which they can access with scaffolding and adaptations where required. Recently, there have been attempts by some historians to release books aimed at young children, such as *Black and British: A short, essential history* by David Olusoga. Just as when we are reading sources, we want our pupils to remember to look for hidden meanings and consider the author and context. You should be cautious of teaching children to search for facts when reading, as in history we read for narrative or argument (Historical Association, 2021a). Before reading in history, you might want to prepare your children by pre-teaching vocabulary or telling the story in an accessible way before looking at more complex texts. Another way you could support pupils with reading in history is to prepare a 'checklist' to consider when reading, including some of the key questions discussed above.

In this section, we have considered how historians read. It is worth noting that reading this way does not have to be contained to history. Reading critically, like we do in history, is crucial when reading in modern life. From newspaper articles and political messaging to social media posts and blogs, we need to be cautious of viewing texts simply as a means of gaining information and consider 'sourcing', 'contextualising', and 'corroborating', just as we do in history. Therefore, reading in history lessons is not just essential for getting better at history but also for preparing pupils for the world in which we live.

Writing like a historian

Writing in history is about so much more than integrating cross-curricular writing initiatives. When children are taught to write historically, they gain insight into how knowledge is constructed and communicated within the discipline. Historical thinking and writing are intrinsically linked (Monte-Sano, 2010). While writing in history requires children to consider general writing practices, such as handwriting and spelling, we also need to consider what makes writing in history different from other subjects.

Historical writing requires pupils to combine their broad historical knowledge and understanding of concepts across historical periods, use precise vocabulary, and apply their disciplinary knowledge to formulate an answer to a question. This is not easy and is not something we should expect pupils to master in primary school. However, this does not mean that you cannot lay the foundations for writing historically. While some teachers might seek to remove or reduce writing demands in history as children find writing hard, it is worth remembering that writing well is essential for success in life (even now that we have AI!). Writing historically is part of learning history. Therefore, you should aim to create a positive writing culture that values writing and sets up all pupils for success. What makes writing challenging is also what makes it rewarding. Writing down our arguments allows us to think more deeply, as our paper can hold more thoughts than we could in our working memory alone (Sealy, 2024). Writing also enables us to organise these thoughts in a way we could not do through speech alone. Therefore, through their written accounts, pupils can think more deeply with their historical knowledge and organise it in new ways to formulate their arguments.

Language and grammar

Quigley argues that writing across the curriculum is challenging as each subject discipline has its own 'chess match' of expectations, vocabulary, and grammar patterns (Quigley, 2022). By explicitly teaching children the language and grammar associated with the discipline, you can prepare them for success in writing in history. Using precise language, punctuation and grammar are not added extras; they are tools for shaping and enhancing a historical argument (Foster, 2015). Here are some examples of the types of language, grammar and writing techniques that can be taught to children.

In practice: using different tenses

WHAT?	WHY ARE THESE USEFUL IN HISTORY?	EXAMPLES
Past tense	As the events they are writing about took place in the past, historians often write in the past tense.	The Great Fire of London **started** in a baker's shop in Pudding Lane.

WHAT?	WHY ARE THESE USEFUL IN HISTORY?	EXAMPLES
Past perfect tense	The past perfect tense describes an action or event that happened before another action or event in the past. This helps historians arrange events in order and draw attention to connections between events.	The Battle of Hastings **has been remembered** as a turning point in Britain's history **since it took place** in 1066.
Adjectives	Adjectives can be used to add descriptions. In history, you can use them to illustrate your argument.	The **influential** leader. The **pivotal** event. The **enduring** impact.
Modal verbs	As historians make interpretations based on partial records, modal verbs can be used to indicate the degree of certainty.	Rosa Parks **might** not have known at the time, but her refusal to give up her seat **would** become a defining moment in the civil rights movement.
Conjunctive adverbs	Historians use conjunctive adverbs to join sentences or clauses to highlight how a sentence adds to or contrasts with the previous sentence, or to emphasise cause and effect.	Adds to: **in addition, moreover, furthermore** Contrasts with: **however, alternatively, in contrast** Cause and effect: **therefore, as a result**
Fronted adverbials	These help historians provide concise additional information about time, place, and manner of frequency.	In Rome, … After the battle, … In 1066, …
Causal connectives	These link cause and effect in a sentence, which is particularly useful when constructing causal arguments.	because of due to as a result of
Subordinate clauses	This is another way that historians can add additional information or context in a concise and formal way.	During the Viking invasion, **which began in the late eighth century,** England faced many attacks on monasteries and settlements.

WHAT?	WHY ARE THESE USEFUL IN HISTORY?	EXAMPLES
Signpost sentences	The sentences at the start and end of the paragraph set out (or 'signposts') the argument.	There were a number of significant changes that took place between the Stone Age and the Bronze Age.

Types of writing in history

The two main types of writing in history, which are not mutually exclusive, are narrative and argument. While younger pupils may be asked to retell historical narratives as simple stories, by Years 5 and 6, children can begin to understand that even narratives in history contain arguments and interpretations. One of the simplest ways of illustrating this is to look at the way in which the characters of the past are portrayed. This is a choice that the historian makes to shape their argument.

One of the main reasons children may be asked to write in history is to answer an enquiry question. To do this, they must argue their claim in response to the question, providing reasons and evidence to justify their response (see Chapter 5). The length and depth of a child's response to an enquiry question will depend on their age, current writing ability, time allocated for writing, and knowledge of history. Answering an enquiry question well requires children to have developed sufficient substantive knowledge of the period and event being studied, and disciplinary knowledge of how historians interpret the past.

While writing extended responses to enquiry questions is a great way of incorporating disciplinary writing, it is not the only way to get children to write in history. Children could also create and annotate timelines, provide summaries, write biographies of key people studied, or write source analyses. It is best to avoid writing activities in history that do not align with the discipline, such as diary entries or creating advertisements. While these types of activities might be part of your English curriculum, engaging with these tasks in history could lead to misconceptions about what historians do.

Teaching writing in history

Just as we have discussed regarding speaking and reading like historians, writing in history needs to be explicitly taught. You need to ensure that you model to pupils what is expected and provide scaffolds for all children to be successful (as discussed in Chapter 5). One way we can do this is to provide well-planned exemplars. You may ask teachers to write these models themselves or provide them. Having a go at the task you are setting pupils is a great way of preparing to teach writing. You can highlight the key points you want pupils to include and the vocabulary and grammar you need to teach explicitly. Providing live modelling to children, as well as modelled outcomes to discuss, can demonstrate the thought process that historians go through when constructing their arguments. You can talk aloud, considering which key points you want to use as evidence, what is most relevant to answer the question, and how you plan to organise your argument. You could give children opportunities to rehearse their arguments in speech first, where they have to justify their arguments to convince their audience. As discussed in Chapter 5, sentence stems, word banks and writing frames are useful scaffolds too. You can use writing frames and word banks to support children in planning out their responses. It is particularly important for Key Stage 2 pupils to be given time to edit and re-draft their responses so that they understand the full writing process.

Case study: inference and finding the hidden meaning

Phil teaches in Year 6. As part of their history curriculum, the school has chosen to teach about World War II. During this topic, Phil decides that he wants to provide opportunities for children to read written sources in more depth. He notices that his pupils are able to extract key information from written sources, but they struggle to infer the meaning behind the words and consider the author or context in which the source was created. Therefore, Phil decides to spend time modelling how to read like a historian (I do), before giving children a go at reading and analysing sources in pairs and feeding back as a class (we do). Once the children have spent time looking at the source together, he then asks them to have a go at independently annotating the source (I do). He asks them to consider what they know about the author, in this case Adolf Hitler, and the 'hidden' meaning behind some of the words. Here is an example of the work that Phil's Year 6 pupils complete:

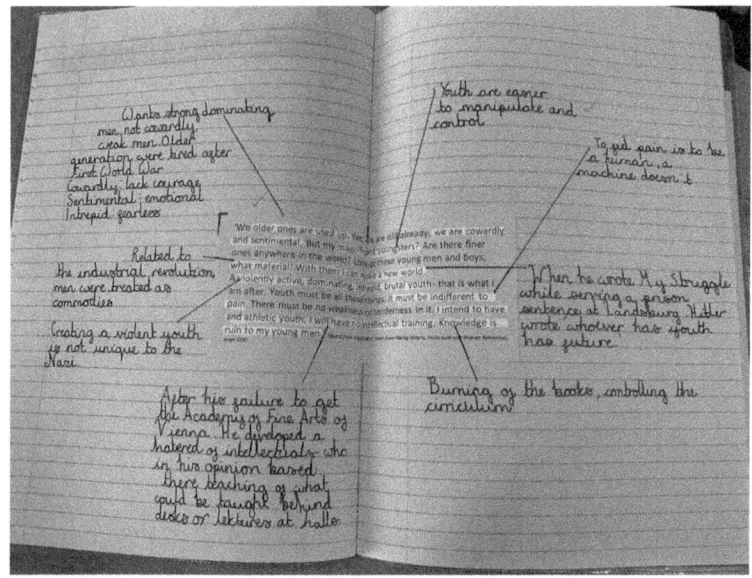

Figure 7.1: An example of Year 6 work

Chapter summary

- Disciplinary literacy refers to how we think, speak, read and write in each subject.

- Each academic discipline has its unique way of creating, communicating and evaluating knowledge.

- Pupils need to be explicitly taught how to communicate in history, including the vocabulary and grammar that historians use.

- 'Oracy' lessons in history should be focused on purposeful and historically valid discussions and debates.

- You need to ensure you set children up for success when speaking, listening, reading and writing in history lessons by establishing clear expectations and using models and scaffolding.

Questions for reflection

- How do we embed disciplinary literacy in our curriculum?
- What opportunities do we provide for children to speak, read and write like historians?
- How do we set pupils up for success when speaking, reading and writing in history?
- What improvements could I make as a history subject leader to improve reading and writing in our school?

Example PD session: disciplinary literacy

Here is an example of what a PD session on disciplinary literacy could look like.

TIMING SUGGESTION	SESSION GUIDANCE
8 mins	Following a training session on substantive and disciplinary knowledge, ask teachers to retrieve knowledge by asking them, 'What is history, and what do historians do?' If teachers are not secure in their disciplinary knowledge, provide an opportunity to discuss this in more detail before looking at disciplinary literacy.
8 mins	Explain what disciplinary literacy is and highlight the importance of disciplinary literacy in primary history, using this chapter and the suggested reading in 'Explore further'.
14 mins	Using this chapter and suggested reading in 'Explore further', explain the ways in which we can explicitly teach pupils to speak, read and write like historians using examples.
15 mins	Teachers can review their curriculum and plan how they will teach pupils to speak, read and write like historians in their next history unit.

Explore further

- Clare Sealy's (2024) article, 'Oracies not oracy', found here: https://primar
ytimery.com/2024/08/25/oracies-not-oracy
- The Historical Association's (2021) article 'What's the wisdom on extended
reading?', found in *Teaching History*, volume 183
- The Historical Association's (2021) article 'What's the wisdom on extended
writing?', *Teaching History*, volume 184

8 Progression and assessment in history

Assessment is at the heart of effective teaching. If you value history as an important subject within the primary curriculum, it is essential to gather evidence to uncover to what extent children remember and understand what has been taught and reflect upon the progress they are making. Assessment can encompass many things and can be best thought of as a set of tools you can use to collect the information you need. When you are considering any form of assessment, it is a good idea to reflect upon its purpose and ask yourself what you would do differently as a result of having this information.

In this chapter, we are going to dive deeper into effective assessment in history and consider:

- what it means to learn more and get better in history.
- what we can learn from what has been tried in the past.
- practical strategies we can use to implement formative assessment in the classroom.

What does it mean to learn more and get better at history?

Before we look more closely at what it means to get better at history, let's take a moment to consider what learning really means. There are several useful definitions to describe learning. One you may be familiar with is that learning is a change in long-term memory. According to prominent cognitive scientists Kirschner et al., the primary aim of teaching should be to 'alter long-term memory' (Kirschner et al. 2006). They argue that nothing has been learned if there has been no change in long-term memory. Another useful definition offered by cognitive psychologists Soderstrom and Bjork (2015) emphasises that the goal of teaching is to 'facilitate long-term learning- that is, to create relatively permanent changes in comprehension, understanding and skills of the types that will support long-term retention and transfer'. This perspective is helpful as it argues that learning is about both remembering and having the flexibility to use and apply what we have learned. This helps us to distinguish between long-term learning, which requires a change in long-term memory, from mere performance. For instance, a child may correctly answer a question related to Henry VIII during their history lesson on Henry VIII. However, the real test is whether they can still recall who he is later on and whether they can use and apply this knowledge, for example, to compare and contrast his reign with that of another monarch being studied.

Therefore, to get better at history, children need to remember both the core substantive and disciplinary knowledge you have taught them and be able to use and apply this knowledge, for example, by constructing arguments, crafting narratives or evaluating sources. You can support children to do this in history by helping them to be able to:

- establish connections between new learning and existing knowledge in long-term memory.

- understand and construct causal arguments to explain why things happened or did not happen and the consequences of this.

- analyse and articulate how and why certain aspects of the past changed or remained constant over time.

- interpret various sources and understand how historians use sources as evidence to support their claims.

- engage with different interpretations of the past and consider how and why people hold differing historical perspectives.

- explain how and why aspects of the past are ascribed historical significance.

The history of assessment in history – what can we learn from the past?

When it comes to education, there is a lot we can learn from looking back at what has been tried before. Learning from the past can help us make better future decisions. Therefore, before exploring the best ways to assess history, let's first reflect on what has been done before.

Back in 1991, the first National Curriculum for History was rolled out in England and Wales. This curriculum established attainment targets and levels designed to emphasise the disciplinary nature of the subject. While the programmes of study did prescribe substantive knowledge, the statements for the levels for each Attainment Target focused on hierarchies of disciplinary thinking, or 'skills', such as, recognising that 'causes can vary in importance'. However, such statements overlooked the fact that an individual's ability to understand and prioritise causes is dependent on their knowledge of the content. In their article, 'What's the wisdom on…history assessment', the Historical Association (2021) argues that these types of statements cannot help us accurately measure progress. This is because determining the significance of a cause can be either straightforward or complex, depending on the depth of the content or the difficulty of the question posed. In addition, the Historical Association argues that the disconnect between knowledge and disciplinary thinking in assessing history led to some unhelpful teaching practices, such as creating 'statement of attainment ladders' for children to memorise, which could have masked an absence of real progress.

The 1995 National Curriculum sought to integrate substantive knowledge back into the assessment process and distinguish between formative and summative assessment.

- **Formative assessment** is ongoing, informal assessments that serve to guide further learning, often referred to as 'assessment *for* learning'
- **Summative assessment** reviews and evaluates learning against a standard or benchmark at the end of a specific period, commonly referred to as 'assessment *of* learning'

The guidance clarified that teachers were to use daily formative assessment to assess what children had learned and rely upon the level descriptors only to establish a 'best fit' for end-of-key-stage summative assessments. However, driven by a demand for internal data, it was not uncommon for these descriptors to be divided into skills hierarchies, applied to individual work (rather than being used for end of key stage assessments) and used by schools to 'measure' progress across the year.

While schools were liberated from these types of level descriptors in 2014, many primary schools are still reflecting on the best way of assessing history. In 2023, the Ofsted subject report, 'Rich encounters with the past', revealed that assessment in history was still underdeveloped in most primary schools they visited. So, what can you do to make sure that history is assessed effectively in your school?

Firstly, you need to understand that without nationally agreed expectations or standardised tests in primary history (like you might use in English, maths, and science) it is not possible to assess whether a child is working 'at,' 'below', or 'above' age-related standards in Key Stage 1 and Key Stage 2. This makes summative assessment tricky as it is challenging to evaluate learning if we have nothing reliable to judge it against. In order to evaluate learning, you must be able to compare it against a standard or benchmark (Sealy, 2022). You could devise your own benchmark and create non-standardised assessments that evaluate how well children are learning your curriculum. However, you must remember that these assessments do not allow you to make inferences about performance beyond your school. You should also make sure that any assessment system you use does not divert significant time away from focusing on teaching and learning, especially as the use of this type of evaluative data is limited.

Today, it is largely agreed that formative assessment is the most useful type of assessment for primary history, as it provides information that can be used to improve learning. Therefore, this chapter will predominantly focus on how we can embed effective formative assessment in our schools.

Assessing in the Early Years

Before we look at formative assessment in history in more detail, let us first take a look at the Early Years. In the Early Years in England, we do have statutory summative assessments, which include as part of the 'Understanding the world' area of learning, that children are expected to recognise some similarities and differences between the past and present, and begin to understand aspects of the past through settings, characters and events they encounter. While pupils do not begin their formal history education until Year 1, as a history subject leader it is important for you to be informed about how well children are learning in the Early Years and how the curriculum and experiences provided to them will help them to achieve this Early Learning Goal. In addition to summative assessments, teachers in the Early Years should also engage in ongoing formative assessment, which can include observations and discussions with the children as well as some of the other techniques we will be discussing in this chapter.

Assessing primary history

What does effective formative assessment look like in practice?

In their subject report, Ofsted (2023) noted that in the best examples of assessment they saw, teachers had a clear, shared understanding of what they wanted pupils to know and focused their assessment on checking they knew it. In other words, to be able to assess well you have to clearly understand what you want children to know and be able to do. This highlights the importance of having a clearly specified curriculum (as discussed in Chapter 4). For example, if I aim for all children to grasp the significance of the introduction of farming during the Neolithic age, I can design my assessments to check every child understands this by the end of the unit. One effective approach to clarify your curriculum is to identify the core knowledge, or endpoints, that you hope all children will fully understand by the end of the unit. These should encompass the most important points and ideally comprise of knowledge that is generative, enabling pupils to build on what they know as they progress through the curriculum. For example, if I am teaching a unit on ancient Egypt, the core knowledge I might identify could be as follows.

1. Know that the ancient Egyptians were an ancient civilisation who lived near the Nile in Egypt, Africa.

2. Understand the significance of their location near the river Nile – the flooding of the Nile created fertile land for growing crops.

3. Know about the hierarchal nature of ancient Egyptian society, and understand some of the ways that life was the same/different for different groups of people at the time (e.g. the Pharaohs, the craftsmen, the farmers and so on).

4. Understand that the ancient Egyptians believed in many gods and goddesses and prepared for the afterlife.

5. Know that archaeologists, such as Zahi Hawass, have made discoveries that have helped us learn more about the ancient Egyptians.

Once you have a clear idea of what you want children to learn, you need to consider the tools you will use to assess their progress. It is always important to think carefully about the purpose of any assessment tools you use. Typically, the three core purposes of assessment in history are:

1. To help **children** remember, connect and apply their knowledge.

2. To assist **teachers** in identifying ways to further support pupils and address any knowledge gaps or misconceptions.

3. To provide information to **leaders** that can be used to enhance the curriculum and improve the overall quality of teaching and learning in history.

Another important aspect to keep in mind is how you will respond to the information gathered during assessments. Ongoing formative assessment necessitates making inferences and taking action to improve learning. We can achieve this by:

- providing effective feedback that motivates pupils and offers clear next steps.
- identifying gaps in knowledge and adapting lessons accordingly.
- addressing and correcting any misconceptions pupils might have.

Effective assessment tools and strategies

Here are some helpful tools and strategies to use when assessing the children in history.

Assessing prior learning

As we have previously discussed, providing opportunities for children to retrieve prior learning enhances the retention and application of knowledge. This can be particularly effective in enabling children to connect new ideas with what they have previously learned. American psychologist Ausubel famously argued that 'The most important single factor influencing learning is what the learner already knows. Ascertain this and teach him accordingly' (Ausubel, 1968). Evidence from neuroscience supports this theory that activating existing knowledge makes the learning process more efficient as new memories integrate with what the person already knows (van Kesteren and Meeter, 2020). Consequently, it is essential for teachers to use assessments to uncover what children know and understand and respond to this information in a meaningful way.

We can do this in a number of ways, including:

- **Questioning techniques:** Using a range of questioning strategies can help elicit what children know and remember. This includes straightforward recall questions such as, 'Who won the Battle of Hastings?' as well as more complex, open-ended questions such as, 'To what extent did life change in Britain during the Industrial Revolution?'. Children can be encouraged to respond in various formats, whether verbally, on mini whiteboards, through interactive quizzes or in their books.

- **Talk partner discussions**: Encouraging children to engage in discussions with their partners allows all children to share their ideas. Teachers can monitor these conversations to identify key points raised that can be addressed as a whole class. This approach can be particularly effective when children are prompted to use subject-specific vocabulary in their discussions, enabling teachers to assess their grasp of keywords in context. If teachers have additional adults in the classroom, they can also help by listening to conversations and feeding back any useful comments.

- **Timeline tasks:** Asking children to draw timelines, or order events on a timeline provided for them, is an effective strategy for developing children's chronological understanding and supporting pupils to relate what they are currently learning with previously studied events and periods. For example, at the beginning of a topic on Anglo-Saxon Britain you could ask children to place some of the time periods they have previously studied (such as the Romans in Britain) on a timeline. This visual representation will help children develop a clearer understanding of the sequence of historical events and periods, thereby strengthening their mental timelines and enabling them to draw connections between what occurred before and after the period currently being studied.

- **Multiple-choice quizzing (MCQs):** Low-stakes MCQs can effectively help children retrieve prior knowledge and uncover misconceptions. It is important that quizzes are not used to memorise trivial disconnected facts but support pupils with retaining core knowledge, such as the names of important people, significant dates or time periods, and key vocabulary and concepts. Regular, informal quizzing can help secure knowledge and can be a fun way of engaging children with their own learning. Children can self-mark, and quiz questions can be revisited to support with long-term learning. If you are using multiple-choice quizzing with younger pupils, it is important you consider the reading ability of all pupils to ensure that quizzes are accessible for all. One way you can do this is to use images and read questions aloud to pupils to access as a whole class.

Assessing learning during lessons

In addition to evaluating what children have learned in previous lessons, it is crucial that you assess what children understand in relation to new knowledge being taught. To do this well, you need to be clear about what you want children to learn during the lesson. Just as when we are assessing prior knowledge, we should employ a range of strategies to check understanding during a lesson, including:

- questioning
- using mini-whiteboards to gather responses from the whole class
- timeline tasks
- talk partner discussions
- written tasks.

The information that teachers collect needs to be acted on. For example, if a misconception arises during a talk partner discussion, it might be beneficial to address this straight away and spend time unpicking it with the whole class. However, this does not mean all issues need to be acted upon immediately. If a teacher discovers that children have not quite grasped an important concept, such as democracy, they may decide to reflect upon this in greater depth after the lesson and use this knowledge to re-plan subsequent lessons to meet pupils' needs.

Ultimately, it is important to remember that when you are teaching history, you are always trying to elicit, understand, and respond to your pupils' developing mental models of the past and of how historians work (Historical Association, 2021c).

Assessing learning across multiple lessons

One of the best ways for pupils to demonstrate their knowledge from a sequence of lessons is by answering a historically-framed enquiry question (as we discussed in Chapter 5). As history teachers, Brown and Burnham said, 'these enquiry-based tasks ensure that assessment is integral to the teaching, bringing together the learning that has taken place' (Brown and Burnham, 2014). When evaluating pupils' responses to these questions, teachers can assess both the substantive and disciplinary knowledge that has been taught. For example, if a child was asked to answer the question, 'To what extent did life change in Britain between the Stone Age and the Iron Age', the child could demonstrate their substantive knowledge by explaining some of the things that changed/ stayed the same during this period, such as the introduction of farming. Pupils could also demonstrate their disciplinary knowledge by including examples of discoveries made by archaeologists, such as Howick House, and explaining how these findings have shaped our understanding of this period. Therefore, a child's response to a question like this can help teachers elicit what children know and understand about the topic and the discipline.

As we have mentioned, effective formative assessment needs to be acted upon. When children answer these questions, it is important that teachers provide effective feedback and use assessments to inform future planning. The feedback we provide children needs to be actionable. For example, asking a child to improve their work by 'organising their ideas more clearly' can be unhelpful. If you notice that the structure of their written responses needs improvement, you can address this through explicit teaching. You should model effective organisation techniques and possibly use appropriate scaffolds, such as writing frames or other support tools.

Using enquiry questions in history enables teachers to identify areas for improvement and supports pupils to think deeply and apply their knowledge, ultimately enhancing learning. The subject leader and the school's leadership team can also use these written responses to evaluate how effectively curriculum aims are being fulfilled. For example, looking at various outcomes from Years 1 to 6, along with other measures such as pupil voice, can provide useful information about how well children are learning your curriculum. This information can help you reflect on what you could do to help improve further.

Case study: retrieval practice and quizzing

Matthew is a subject leader in a primary in the Southwest. The school has recently developed a well-sequenced knowledge-rich curriculum in history. However, during both a learning walk and pupil voice, Matthew identifies that children struggle to remember what they have learned previously, and teachers rarely ask children to connect prior knowledge with new learning. Like many schools, he is looking at ways of using formative assessment strategies to improve learning in history. The school recently received training on the benefits of using retrieval practice as a learning tool. While the main aim of retrieval practice is to retrieve information from the long-term memory to improve recall and long-term retention, it can also help children with transferring knowledge to new contexts and provide valuable information to teachers. He notes that while some teachers attempt to use retrieval practice in history, for example, short MCQs to check what children could remember from previous lessons, the questions are not always well thought-through and often require children to remember trivial disconnected facts that are not relevant to new learning. Matthew decides that improving the use of quizzing is a goal for his action plan as this is something that is already happening in school but is not being used effectively in history. He leads a staff training session for teachers on how to improve the use of quizzing in history.

During his staff meeting, he gives examples of how teachers can use effective quiz questions to elicit possible errors and misconceptions, which can be addressed as a class. For example:

'How do historians use sources?'

A: Historians only use sources written at the time because they are the most reliable.

B: Historians use a range of sources and interpret them critically to construct their claims (correct answer).

C: Historians use evidence to uncover facts that can tell us a true account of exactly what happened in the past.

He explains that this is an effective example because the incorrect answers in this quiz can elicit common misconceptions and errors, such as 'only sources written at the time are reliable' and 'there is one true account of the past that historians seek to discover'.

Following his training session, he creates a 'top tips for using quizzing in history' document as a reminder for teachers to refer to during their PPA and provides extra support for teachers with implementing this in their classes. Over the year, Matthew uses a range of strategies to monitor the use of quizzing such as planning reviews, learning walks and pupil voice. He then decides to introduce other ways of using retrieval practice in history beyond the use of a quiz. He considers how these strategies could be useful for formative assessment as well as tools for improving learning.

Reporting to parents and carers

Finally it is important to consider, as a school, how you will communicate to parents and carers about their child's learning in history. Since there are no statutory assessments for history in Key Stage 1 or Key Stage 2 and we do not have any standardised tests available, you cannot present parents and carers with a level or judgement based on an age-related expectation, such as 'working below, above, or at the expected standard.' Instead, you can provide insights into how their child is performing in relation to the expectations set out in your school's history curriculum. When engaging with parents and carers, it may be helpful to reflect on the following questions:

- How well is the child learning your curriculum?
- Are there any specific aspects of the curriculum that the child is finding particularly challenging?
- How actively do they contribute during lessons?
- Are they able to complete tasks independently, or do they require additional support?
- Can you share an example of an impressive piece of work or an interesting contribution made by the child in class?
- Which parts of the curriculum have they particularly enjoyed?
- How can parents and carers support their child's learning at home?

While it may not be feasible to set specific history targets for parents and carers to work on with their child, you could encourage them to assist with quizzing at home or help their child learn key vocabulary from their knowledge organiser (if this is something that your school does). If the child has a keen interest in an aspect of history, you may want to inform parents and carers and suggest ways they can further nurture their child's curiosity, such as visiting a local museum or exploring historical literature together.

Top tips for assessment in history

DO	DON'T
Focus on your curriculum – you need to be clear about what you want pupils to know and remember, or you cannot assess whether children are meeting these expectations.	Try to disconnect and assess discrete 'skills' in history. Remember, statements like 'I can identify different causes' can be made more or less difficult based on the content being studied.
Use retrieval practice as a low-stakes learning tool. This tool can support children in connecting prior knowledge to new learning and can also be used for formative assessment.	Use retrieval practice to memorise random facts. Consider what you want children to learn and focus on retrieval of core knowledge.
Focus on ongoing, low-stakes formative assessment.	Focus on one form of assessment only.
Adopt a variety of approaches, including utilising oral responses through questioning and the use of talk partners, as well as longer written responses.	Adopt a tick-box approach with 'I can' statements – these do not appreciate the complexity of progression in history.
Involve the children. For example, they can mark their own MCQs and be expected to action their feedback.	Provide generic feedback that is challenging for children to action.
Make sure you think deeply about the purpose of assessment and act upon it.	Adopt a time-consuming approach that increases workload with little impact on learning.
Look at the bigger picture, not just individual performance. How can you use assessment to provide you with information to improve the curriculum and/or improve teaching and learning?	Confuse the purpose of assessment with 'proving' progress for external validation, e.g. Ofsted, or use it as part of a high-stakes accountability measure.

Chapter summary

- Assessment is at the heart of effective teaching.
- Assessment can be best thought of as a set of tools you can use to collect the information you need to act upon.
- You must carefully consider the purpose of any assessment strategy you intend to use.

Questions for reflection

- To what extent does our curriculum clearly specify the journey that pupils go on to improve in history? Is there anything I could do to improve it?
- How do we assess in history?
- How do teachers use information gathered by assessments?
- In what ways could we use assessment more effectively in our school?

Example PD session: embedding effective formative assessment

Here is an example of what a PD session on effective formative assessment could look like.

TIMING SUGGESTION	SESSION GUIDANCE
10 mins	Revisit prior learning on the importance of sequencing the curriculum and share some examples from your history curriculum.
10 mins	Read Michael Fordham's blog on the curriculum as the progression model: https://clioetcetera.com/2020/02/08/what-did-i-mean-by-the-curriculum-is-the-progression-model/ Think about ways we can ensure that children are learning what we set out for them in the curriculum.

TIMING SUGGESTION	SESSION GUIDANCE
15 mins	In year groups, key stages, or as a whole school, share some examples of how you assess history.
20 mins	Give teachers time to reflect on their plans for the next few weeks. Spend time thinking about how you will embed effective formative assessment into lessons.

Explore further

- Michael Fordham's (2020) blog on the curriculum as the progression model: https://clioetcetera.com/2020/02/08/what-did-i-mean-by-the-curriculum-is-the-progression-model/

- Daisy Christodoulou's (2017) book: *Making Good Progress?: the future of Assessment for Learning*

- Richard Selfridge and James Pembroke's (2022) book: *Dataproof Your School: how to use assessment data effectively*

9 Implementing change

Improving the quality of teaching and learning in history at your school is a key priority of every subject leader. To make this happen, you will likely be required to produce an action or development plan to support the subject's strategic development. Your action plan should include:

- the key priorities you wish to focus on (three priorities should be enough; more than that can become challenging to enact).
- actions you plan to take, with clear timescales.
- success criteria to identify how you will show that your priority has been successfully implemented.

This chapter will support you with creating and implementing your action plan following the Education Endowment Foundation (EEF) guidance on implementation. Implementation is the process of implementing a decision or plan. Another way to think of it is bridging the gap between what you know and what you do. Therefore, this chapter will serve as a useful guide to help you put some of what you have learned in this book into action!

In this chapter, we will:

- learn how to plan for success by avoiding common pitfalls.
- use the EEF guidance to help us explore, prepare, deliver and sustain our new strategies.
- reflect upon what this will look like in our school by learning from practical case studies of action plans in other primary schools.

Planning for success

Implementing a new approach successfully is not easy or straightforward. There will always be barriers to effectively implementing your action plan. Schools are busy, complex places, and competing pressures make driving and sustaining change hard. There are many reasons why well-intentioned plans fail to embed successfully. Here are just some of the common reasons given by leaders.

- The school has failed to pinpoint the right areas for improvement and/or the best way to address them.
- Teachers were not engaged during the process and were not given the chance to discuss their perspectives or concerns before the plan was put into action.
- Leaders have not actively participated in motivating and guiding the change, so the plan lacks the guidance needed to remain on track.
- A school is trying to implement too many things simultaneously.
- The priorities do not align with the school development plan.
- Not enough time has been devoted to knowledge building with teachers first, so they are not confident in implementing the change.
- The priority is too wide-ranging, and the success criteria are not sufficiently detailed for staff to identify impact.
- The priority is generic and does not consider the school's context.

The EEFs Guide to Implementation

The EEF's guidance report, 'A School's Guide to Implementation', states that implementation is a collaborative and social process (Sharples et al, 2024). Their guidance sets out three key elements that enable effective implementation in schools:

1. The **behaviours** that drive effective implementation.
2. The **contextual factors** that influence implementation.
3. A **structured, but flexible, process** to enact implementation.

In the next section, we will focus on the processes that help schools enact implementation through the phases of 'explore,' 'prepare,' 'deliver' and 'sustain.' Before we look at these in more depth, it is important to consider the cross-cutting behavioural and contextual factors needed to successfully implement a plan.

Recommendation 1: adopt the behaviours that drive effective implementation

Implementation is fundamentally a collaborative and social process driven by how people think, behave, and interact (Moore et al, 2024). These behaviours are at the heart of successful implementation:

	What does it mean?	Questions to consider
Engage	Engage people so they can shape what happens while also providing overall direction.	How will you involve leaders, teachers, TAs, parents, carers and pupils to understand what you are attempting to change in history and why? How will you ensure everyone understands your plan and what it will look like in practice?
Unite	Unite people around what is being implemented, how it will be implemented, and why it matters.	How will you explore common views and values to unite teachers and improve buy-in? How will you unite teachers through a shared understanding of what is being implemented, how it will be implemented and why?
Reflect	Reflect, monitor, and adapt to improve implementation.	Have you reflected on the needs of pupils and staff when considering your approach? How have you reflected on the school's context when considering the feasibility of your plan?

Case study: engaging the team

After reviewing her school's curriculum, Taraji identified the need for children to learn more about local history. Taraji has read the EEF report and understands that implementation is a collaborative and social process. She wants to ensure that all stakeholders feel valued, listened to, and understand the changes she wants to make and why. To try and get all staff on board, Taraji invites a local historian in to share with the staff how the town was originally a major Viking trading hub. She then shares some pupil voice responses where children said that they do not think their town is important. She gives staff twenty minutes to research for themselves interesting historical facts about their town and then asks for these to be shared. Staff feel excited about sharing more local history with their pupils as a result.

Recommendation 2: attend to the contextual factors that influence implementation

The second important factor to consider when implementing change is your context. The behaviours that drive implementation, which we discussed above, are influenced by what is being implemented, the existing systems and structures and where there are people in place who can enable change.

	What does it mean?	Questions to consider
What is being implemented?	Consider whether what is being implemented is evidence-informed, right for the setting, and manageable to implement.	Is the approach you wish to implement well specified? Is there evidence to support your approach? Is there evidence that the approach worked well in similar settings? Is the approach feasible to implement?
Systems and structures	Develop an infrastructure that supports implementation, for example, time allocation and data systems.	Is there time in the school timetable to implement your approach? Are there monitoring systems in place to reflect upon the implementation process? Do you have the resources you need?
People who enable change	Ensure people who enable change can support, lead, and positively influence implementation.	Who will be available to lead the implementation? Is anyone available to support with the implementation?

It is important to remember that implementing your action plan does not happen in a vacuum. Considering these behaviours and contextual factors when embarking on the implementation process will support you when engaging with the implementation process.

Recommendation 3: use a structured but flexible implementation process

The final recommendation from the EEF provides a process to help schools implement change while applying the behaviours and contextual factors needed for success.

This process includes a set of practical strategies that are organised into four flexible phases:

- explore
- prepare
- deliver
- sustain

We will look at each phase in-depth and then use a case study to help us consider what this may look like in practice.

1. Explore

Before you begin writing an action plan, you first need to identify what needs to change and why. During the 'explore' phase, asking lots of questions and being curious will help you identify development needs. It is important to consider a wide range of information when making decisions, such as assessment data, lesson visits, pupil voice and book looks. Once you have gathered a range of data (as none of these examples are sufficient on their own), you can interpret and reflect upon what is likely to be the root cause of the problem you have identified. Make sure you consider more than just obvious causes. For example, issues with using historical sources could be caused by multiple factors, including pupils' reading ability, the curriculum, or teachers' subject knowledge.

2. Prepare

Once you have identified a problem you want to solve, it is important that you spend time preparing how you will implement your plan rather than jumping straight in. During the 'prepare' phase, you need to take time to plan out your implementation journey clearly. This is essential in laying the groundwork for successful implementation. This will include creating an action plan which should include:

- what you intend to change and why.

- precisely what you plan to do.

- how it will be implemented – professional development (PD), resources and timescales.

- consideration of how you will monitor how well implementation is going.

- the final intended outcomes clearly specified so you will be able to evaluate the impact of changes made.

Once you have completed your plan, you need to consider the practical preparations that need to take place, including:

- **Preparing people**: some people are more resistant to change than others. We must consider how we can bring all staff along with us when implementing something new. You may also wish to identify 'champions' for your approach to positively influence others to support the change.

- **Preparing the approach**: before implementing change, it is important to consider your context and whether adaptations will need to be made.

- **Professional development**: effective professional development can unite staff's knowledge, skills and practices, which supports the implementation of a new approach (Moore et al., 2024).
- **Systems and structures**: ensure the necessary systems and structures are in place to enable success. For example, will staff have the time and resources they need to implement the change?

3. Deliver

When introducing new ways of working, new behaviours need to be learned, and old habits need to be set aside. This can be hard, so it is important to bring staff along with you and enable ongoing improvement by:

- encouraging feedback, including short surveys and open discussions, to find out how things are going and solve any problems that might arise.
- motivating staff by sharing the impact of the approach so far and celebrating great practice.
- managing expectations and letting staff know that change is a process and that impact won't be seen overnight.
- reinforcing initial professional development by providing ongoing support to help embed new skills, knowledge and behaviours.

4. Sustain

In schools, we can feel pressured to make changes and deliver results quickly. While this is sometimes necessary, allowing time for new practices to embed is important. You must be careful not to jump from one new initiative to another, focus on sustaining your approach, and adapt implementation plans where necessary to see long-term improvements. During the 'sustain' phase, you might think about:

- refreshing professional development.
- reviewing and reflecting upon the impact of your approach.
- revisiting your implementation plan to see if it needs amending.
- making the outcomes of the initiative visible to staff and the school community.

- scaling up your initiative, such as implementing it in more classes or more subjects.

- de-implementing an approach if it is not having a positive impact and/or diverting time and resources away from a more pressing need.

Case study: improving the effectiveness of the history curriculum

Fay is an experienced subject leader in a two-form entry primary school in Cambridgeshire. In October, following a visit from a local authority advisor, the senior leadership team raise concerns with Fay about the effectiveness of the history curriculum.

Explore

To learn more about the problem, Fay conducts a book look and pupil voice, carries out a learning walk, looks at curriculum planning and resources, and speaks with her colleagues. Individual teachers have developed the curriculum at her school over time, resulting in a lack of coherent sequencing. In addition, children repeat aspects of the curriculum (they study the Romans as part of a topic in Year 3 and Year 6) and miss out on some key areas of the National Curriculum.

Fay enhances her understanding of effective curriculum design by reading this book as well as some of the recommended texts and considering the advice from the Historical Association. She concludes that the school would benefit from adopting a new curriculum. After speaking with the senior leadership team, they decide that Fay does not have the time to write a new curriculum from scratch and that the school could benefit from adopting a scheme. Two local schools are following different schemes that offer to share their experiences.

Fay decides to visit the local schools to observe their curriculum in action and speak with their staff. The headteacher suggests that Fay brings a couple of teachers with her on the visit. She chooses to bring one teacher who is really optimistic about the change and could champion the new curriculum back at school. She also decides to bring along one teacher who is the most reluctant to change to ensure she is engaged in the decision-making process.

During the visit, all three teachers were impressed with the schemes being taught. However, one school had a more similar context to Fay's school, and their scheme aligned more closely with their school values and would fit with their timetable and budget. Fay decides that she would like to implement this scheme back in her school.

Prepare

Now that Fay has identified the problem and how she plans to solve it, she needs to prepare to put her plan into action. She began preparing staff at her school when she organised her visits. Next, she needs to share her plan with the rest of her colleagues. To do this well, she carefully plans her approach to implementing this change and speaks to her senior leadership team about leading a training session in January to share this with staff. There is no one agreed way of writing an action plan, so Fay uses the template her senior leadership team provide. Here is a copy of Fay's action plan:

Priority: To implement a coherent, well-sequenced history curriculum to ensure that all children know more, and remember more, in history.

Actions	Timescale	Monitoring and responsibilities
Fay will adapt the new scheme to incorporate local history elements.	December	SLT and Fay
Fay and the two teachers who attended the visit will try one of the new units in their classes.	Autumn B	SLT and Fay will observe lessons, look at books, and conduct a pupil voice in December to reflect upon the effectiveness of the implementation to date.
Fay will lead a short session with staff to introduce the new scheme, providing a clear rationale for why and how the scheme will be implemented and teachers will be given time to look at the new plans.	January INSET	Fay

Fay will speak with the organisation that provides the plans and staff to decide which units staff will teach from Spring B onwards.	January	Fay
Teachers will receive training provided by the organisation that wrote the scheme on how to enact the curriculum.	February	Fay, SLT
Fay will lead a session to parents and carers outlining their new curriculum.	February	Fay
All teachers will begin using the amended scheme.	Spring B – Summer B	SLT and Fay conduct learning walks, pupil voice interviews and book reviews at the end of the term to assess the effectiveness of the implementation to date.
Fay will provide a staff survey for feedback on the new curriculum.	Summer A	Survey responses shared with SLT
Further professional development will be provided to teachers and any issues raised from the survey will be addressed.	Summer B	Fay

Deliver

Following the completion of the action plan and trials in three classes in the school, Fay and her school are ready to enter the 'deliver' stage of her plan (outlined in the action plan above). This phase includes sharing positive outcomes from the classes involved in the trial, providing professional development and asking for feedback.

Sustain

Fay understands that embedding a new curriculum takes time. Feedback from teachers in the summer term is generally positive and information collected via learning walks, pupil voice interviews and book looks show that the curriculum is being followed effectively. Next academic year, Fay plans to provide further professional development to ensure the effective delivery of the new curriculum.

Chapter summary

- Successful implementation requires careful planning, including identifying priorities, making evidence-informed decisions, assessing school readiness, and developing a clear implementation plan.
- The EEF guidance report sets out three elements that enable effective implementation in schools: behaviours, contextual factors, and a structured, but flexible, process.
- The EEF's four-stage process for implementing change in schools is a useful model from which to work.
- The EFF process includes four phases: explore, prepare, deliver and sustain.

Questions for reflection

- How do I currently identify priorities for improvement in my school, and how can I use a more data-driven approach during this process?
- How do I plan professional development to support the implementation of our priorities? What conversations do I need to have with my headteacher/school leadership team to support me with this?
- Are there some priorities that have not been embedded as I anticipated? Can I identify the reasons for this? What steps do I need to take now?
- What professional development do I need to support me in leading history?

Explore further

- The EEF's (2024) *A School's Guide to Implementation* by Sharples et al.

Bibliography

Adcock, S. (2021), 'Curriculum: The mirror and the window'. *Steve Adcock blog*, https://stevea dcock81.wordpress.com/2021/06/01/curriculum-the-mirror-and-the-window

Agarwal, P. K., Nunes, L.D. and Blunt, J. R. (2021), 'Retrieval practice consistently benefits student learning: A systematic review of applied research in schools and classrooms'. *Educational Psychology Review* 33.4: 1409–1453.

Archer, A.L. and Hughes, C.A. (2011), *The Power of Explicit Teaching and Direct Instruction*. London: Sage Publications Ltd.

Arnold, M. (1869), *Culture and Anarchy: An Essay in Political and Social Criticism*. London: Macmillan.

Ashby, R. (2011), 'Understanding historical evidence: teaching and learning challenges' in Ian Davies (ed) *Debates in History Teaching*. Abingdon: Routledge, pp137–147.

Ausubel, D.P. (1968), *Educational Psychology: A Cognitive View*. New York: Holt, Rinehart and Winston.

Baddeley, A.D. and Hitch, D. (1974), 'Working Memory'. *Psychology of Learning and Motivation*, 8: 47–89.

Bartlett, F. C. (1932), *Remembering: A study in experimental and social psychology*. Cambridge: Cambridge University Press.

Bernstein, B.B. (2000), *Pedagogy, Symbolic Control, and Identity: Theory, research, critique*. Lanham: Rowman and Littlefield.

Boxer, A. (ed) (2019), *The ResearchEd Guide to Explicit and Direct Instruction*. London: John Catt.

Boyne, J. (2006), *The Boy in the Striped Pyjamas*. Oxford: David Fickling Books.

Bransford, J. Brown, J.D. Cocking, RR (2000), *How people learn: brain, mind, experience, and school*. Washington: National Academy Press.

Byrom, J. Riley, M. (2008), 'Professional wrestling in the history department: a case study in planning the teaching of the British Empire at Key stage 3', *Teaching History*, 99: 6–14

Carr, E.H. (1961), *What Is History?* London: Penguin Books.

Carr, H. and Lipscombe, S. (2021), *What is History, Now?* London: Weidenfeld and Nicolson.

Chapman, A. (2011), 'Historical interpretations' in Ian Davies (ed) *Debates in History Teaching*, Abingdon: Routledge, pp.96–108.

Chapman, A. (2017), 'Causal Explanation' in Ian Davies (ed) *Debates in History Teaching* (2nd Edition). Abingdon: Routledge, pp.130–143.

Christodoulou, D. (2017), *Making good progress?: the Future of Assessment for Learning*. Oxford: Oxford University Press.

Coe, R., Fitzgibbon, C., and Gregorio, M. (2014), 'What makes great teaching? Review of the underpinning research'. *Sutton Trust*, https://www.suttontrust.com/our-research/great-teaching/.

Cooke, S. (2009), 'The language demands of history'. *National Association for Language Development in the Curriculum*, https://www.naldic.org.uk/Resources/NALDIC/Teach

ing%20and%20Learning/Documents/The%20language%20demands%20of%20Hist ory.pdf.

Corfield, P.J. (2009), 'Teaching history's big pictures: including continuity as well as change', *Teaching History*, 136: 53–59.

Counsell, C. (2005), 'Looking through a Josephine-Butler-shaped window: focusing pupils' thinking on historical significance'. *Teaching History*, 114: 30–36

Counsell, C. (2018), 'Senior Curriculum Leadership 1: The indirect manifestation of knowledge: (A) curriculum as narrative.' *The Dignity of the Thing*, https://thedignityofthe thingblog.wordpress.com/2018/04/07/senior-curriculum-leadership-1-the-indirect-manife station-of-knowledge-a-curriculum-as-narrative/.

Counsell, C. (2018a), 'Taking curriculum seriously', *Impact*, https://my.chartered.college/imp act_article/taking-curriculum-seriously/.

Counsell, C. (2021), 'History' in Cuthbert, A.S. and Standish, A. (eds), *What Should Schools Teach?: Disciplines, subjects and the pursuit of truth* (2nd edition). London: UCL Press, pp. 154–173.

Counsell, C. (2023), 'Laughing muppets, lost memories and lethal mutations: rescuing assessment from knowledge-rich gone wrong'. *Teaching History*, 193: 8–25.

Cowan, N. (2010), 'The Magical Mystery Four: How is Working Memory Capacity Limited, and Why?' *Curr Dir Psychol Sci*, 19(1):51–57.

Davies, I. (ed) (2017), *Debates in History Teaching* (2nd edition). Abingdon: Routledge

Dawson, I. (2004), 'Time for chronology? Ideas for developing chronological understanding', *Teaching History*, 117: 14–24.

De Bruyckere, P., Kirschner, P. and Hulshof, C. (2015), *Urban Myths and Learning and Education*. London: Elsevier.

Department for Education (DfE) (2013), *The national curriculum in England: key stages 1 and 2 framework*. https://www.gov.uk/government/publications/national-curriculum-in-engl and-primary-curriculum.

Department for Education (DfE) (2023), *Early years foundation stage statutory framework. For group and school-based providers*. https://www.gov.uk/government/publications/ early-years-foundation-stage-framework--2

Didau, D. and Rose, N. (2016), *What Every Teacher Needs To Know About Psychology*. London: John Catt.

Ebbinghaus, H. (1885), *Memory: a contribution to experimental psychology*. New York, NY: Dover.

Elton, G.R. (1967), *The Practice of History*. Malden: Blackwell Publishers.

Fletcher-Wood, H. (2018), *Responsive Teaching: Cognitive science and formative assessment in practice*. Abingdon: Routledge

Fordham, M. (2014), 'Making History Stick Part 2: Switching the scale between overview and depth'. *Clio et cetera*, https://clioetcetera.com/2014/08/06/making-history-stick-part-2- switching-the-scale-between-overview-and-depth/.

Fordham, M. (2017), 'What sorts of substantive knowledge are needed to get better at history?' *Clio et cetera*, https://clioetcetera.com/2017/03/21/what-sorts-of-substantive-knowle dge-are-needed-to-get-better-at-history/.

Fordham, M. (2020), 'What did I mean by 'the curriculum is the progression model?' *Clio et cetera*, https://clioetcetera.com/2020/02/08/what-did-i-mean-by-the-curriculum-is-the-progression-model.

Foster, R. (2013), 'The more things change, the more they stay the same: Developing students' thinking about historical change and continuity'. *Teaching History*, 151: 8–17.

Foster, R. (2015), 'Pipe's punctuation and making complex historical claims: how the direct teaching of punctuation can improve students' historical thinking and written argument', *Teaching History*, 159: 8–13.

Gathercole, S. and Alloway, T. (2004), 'Working memory and classroom learning' in *Applied Cognitive Research in K-3 Classrooms*. Abingdon: Routledge.

Graesser, A. Singer, M. and Trabasso T, (1994) 'Constructing Inferences During Narrative Text Comprehension', *Psychological Review*, 101: 371–395.

Guyver, R. (2000), 'History teaching, pedagogy, curriculum and politics: dialogues and debates in regional, national, transnational, international and supernational settings', *International Journal of Historical Learning, Teaching and Research* 11.2.

Hammond, K. (2014), 'The knowledge that 'flavours a claim: towards building and assessing historical knowledge on three scales' *Teaching History*, 157:18–24.

Hanover, V. (1870), Letter from Queen Victoria to Mr. Theodore Martin, May 29, 1870, RA VIC/MAIN/Y/168/29.

Hill, M. (2020), 'Curating the imagined past: world building in the history curriculum'. *Teaching History*, 180:10–20.

Historical Association (2019), 'What's the wisdom on causation?' *Teaching History*, 175:24–27.

Historical Association (2019a), 'What's the wisdom on interpretations of the past?' *Teaching History*, 177: 23–27.

Historical Association (2020), 'What's the wisdom on enquiry questions?' *Teaching History*, 178:16- 19.

Historical Association (2020a), 'What's the wisdom on similarity and difference?' *Teaching History*, 180:52–56.

Historical Association (2020b), 'what's the wisdom on historical significance?' *Teaching History*, 181:50–54.

Historical Association (2021), 'What's the wisdom on consequence?' *Teaching History*, 182:50–53.

Historical Association (2021a), 'What's the wisdom on extended reading?' *Teaching History*, 183:44–47.

Historical Association (2021b) 'What's the wisdom on extended writing?', *Teaching History*, 184:50–56.

Historical Association (2021c), 'What's the wisdom on history assessment?', *Teaching History*, 185:56–59 .

Howard, K. and Hill, C. (2020), *Symbiosis: the curriculum and the classroom*. London: John Catt.

Jenkins, K. (1991), *Re-thinking History*. Abingdon: Routledge.

Jenkins, S. (2018), *A short history of Europe: from Pericles to Putin*. London: Viking.

Karpicke, J. D. and Aue, W. R. (2015), 'The testing effect is alive and well with complex materials'. *Educational Psychology Review*, 27: 317–326.

Karpicke, J. D., Lehman, M., & Aue, W. R. (2014), 'Retrieval-based learning: An episodic context account' in B. H. Ross (ed) *The Psychology of Learning and Motivation*. London: Elsevier Academic Press, pp. 237–284.

Kerr, J. (1971), *When Hitler Stole Pink Rabbit*. London: Collins.

Kirby, J. (2015), 'Knowledge Organisers'. *Joe Kirby* blog, https://joe-kirby.com/2015/03/28/knowledge-organisers/

Kirschner, P.A. Sweller, J. and Clark, R.E. (2006), 'Why Minimal Guidance During Instruction Does Not Work: An Analysis of the Failure of Constructivist, Discovery, Problem-Based, Experiential, and Inquiry-Based Teaching'. *Educational Psychologist*, 41:2, 75–86.

Kirschner, P. and Hendrick, C. (2020), *How Learning Happens: Seminal Works in Educational Psychology and What They Mean in Practice*. Abingdon: Routledge.

Lang, S. (1993), 'What is bias?', *Teaching History*, 73:9–13.

Lang, S. (2003), 'Narrative: the under-rated skill.' *Teaching History*, 110:8–17.

LeCocq, H. (2000), 'Beyond bias: making source evaluation meaningful to Year 7', *Teaching History*, 99: 50–55.

Lee, P. (2011), 'History education and historical literacy' in Ian Davies (ed) *Debates in History Teaching*. Abingdon: Routledge, pp.63–72.

Levstik, L. S. (1995), 'Narrative Constructions: Cultural Frames for History'. *Social Studies*, 86: 113–117.

Lubbock, J. (1865), *Pre-historic Times*. London: Williams and Norgate.

Major, L. and Higgins, S. (2019), *What works?: Research and evidence for successful teaching*. London: Bloomsbury Education.

Mar, R.A., Li, J., Nguyen, A.T.P. et al. (2021), 'Memory and comprehension of narrative versus expository texts: A meta-analysis.' *Psychonomic Bulletin Review* 28:732–749.

Marincola, J. (2001), *Greek Historians*. Oxford: Oxford University Press.

Monte-Sano, C. (2010), 'Disciplinary Literacy in History: An Exploration of the Historical Nature of Adolescents' Writing'. *The Journal of the Learning Sciences*, 19(4): 539–568.

Moore, D., Proctor, R., Benham-Clarke, S., Gains, H., Melendez-Torres, G. J., Axford, N., Rogers, M., Anderson, R., Hall, D., Hawkins, J., Berry, V., Forbes, C. and Lloyd, J. (2024), 'Review of Evidence on Implementation in Education'. *Education Endowment Foundation*. https://educationendowmentfoundation.org.uk/education-evidence/evidence-reviews/implementation-in-education

Mortimore, K. (2020), *Disciplinary Literacy and Explicit Vocabulary Teaching*. London: John Catt.

Morton, D. (2000), Teaching and Learning History in Canada in Stearns, P.N., Seixas, P. and Wineburg, S. (eds) *Knowing, teaching and learning in history: national and international perspectives*. New York: New York University Press, pp51–62.

Munslow, A. (2018), *Narrative and History*. London: Bloomsbury.

Myatt, M. (2018), *The Curriculum: Gallimaufry to Coherence*. London: John Catt.

Navey, M,A. (2018), 'Dealing with the consequences: What do we want students to do with consequence in history?', *Teaching History*, 172:40–49.

Ofsted (2021), 'Research Review Series: History'. *Ofsted*, https://www.gov.uk/government/publications/research-review-series-history/research-review-series-history.

Ofsted (2023), 'Rich encounters with the past: history subject report'. *Ofsted*, https://www.gov.uk/government/publications/subject-report-series-history/rich-encounters-with-the-past-history-subject-report.

Palek, D. (2015), 'What exactly is parliament?' finding the place of substantive knowledge in history', *Teaching History*, 158: 18–25.

Partington, G. (1980), 'What History Should We Teach?', *Oxford Review of Education*, 6(2): 157–176.

Pashler, H. et al (2007), *Organizing Instruction and Study to Improve Student Learning*. Washington, DC: US Department of Education.

Pavio, A. (1971), *Imagery and verbal processes*. New York: Holt, Rinehart and Winston.

Pavio, A. (1986), *Mental representations: A dual coding approach*. Oxford: Oxford University Press.

Pearce, J. (2022), *What every teacher needs to know: How to embed evidence-informed teaching and learning in your school*. London: Bloomsbury.

Phillips, R. (2002), 'Historical significance – the forgotten 'key element'?', *Teaching History*, 106: 14–19.

Quigley, A. (2018), *Closing the Vocabulary Gap*. Abingdon: Routledge.

Quigley, A. (2022), *Closing the Writing Gap*. Abingdon: Routledge.

Randall, R. (2019), 'The Problem with 'The Boy in the Striped Pyjamas" on *Holocaust Centre North blog*. https://holocaustcentrenorth.org.uk/blog/the-problem-with-the-boy-in-the-striped-pyjamas/.

Riley, M. (1997), 'Big stories and big pictures: making outlines and overviews interesting', *Teaching History*, 88: 20–22.

Riley, M. (2008), 'Into the Key Stage 3 history garden: choosing and planting your enquiry questions', *Teaching History*, 99: 8–13.

Robinson, M. (2022), *Curriculum Revolutions: a Practical Guide to Enhancing What you Teach*. London: John Catt.

Rosenshine, B. (2012), 'Principles of instruction: Research-based strategies that all teachers should know', *American Educator*, 36(1): 12–19, 39.

Sealy, C. (2022), 'Don't mix the six! Thinking about assessment as six different tools with six different jobs'. *Primary Timery*, https://primarytimery.com/2022/05/02/dont-mix-the-six-thinking-about-assessment-as-six-different-tools-with-six-different-jobs/.

Sealy, C. (2024), 'Oracies not oracy'. *Primary Timery*, https://primarytimery.com/2024/08/25/oracies-not-oracy/.

Sealy, C. (2024), 'Understanding oracy, understanding writing' *Primary Timery*, https://primarytimery.com/2024/06/21/talking-floats-on-a-sea-of-write/

Selfridge, R. and Pembroke, J. (2022), *Dataproof Your School: How to Use Assessment Data Effectively*. London: Sage Publishing.

Sharples, J., Eaton, J. and Boughelaf, J. (2024), *A School's Guide to Implementation: Guidance Report*. London: Education Endowment Foundation.

Shemilt, D. (1980), *History 13–16 Evaluation Study: Schools Council History 13–16 Project*. Edinburgh: Holmes McDougall.

Shemilt, D. (2000), 'The Caliph's Coin: The Currency of Narrative Frameworks in History Teaching' in Stearns, P.N., Seixas, P. and Wineburg, S. (eds) *Knowing, Teaching and Learning in History: National and International Perspectives.* New York: New York University Press, pp.83–101.

Sisti, H.M, Glass, A.L and Shors, T.J. (2007), 'Neurogenesis and the spacing effect: learning over time enhances memory and the survival of new neurons'. *Learning Memory*, May 10;14(5):368–75.

Soderstrom N.C. and Bjork R A. (2015), 'Learning versus performance: an integrative review.' *Perspectives on Psychological Science.* Mar;10(2):176–99.

Staley, D. J. (2020), *Historical Imagination.* Abingdon: Routledge.

Stenhouse, L. (1975), *An Introduction to Curriculum Research and Development.* London: Heinemann.

Sullivan, D. (2018), 'DfE clarifies reference to enquiry-based learning'. *History,* https://www.history.org.uk/ha-news/categories/455/news/3613/dfe-clarifies-reference-to-enquiry-based-learning.

Sundararajan, N. and Adesope, O. (2020), 'Keep it Coherent: A Meta-Analysis of the Seductive Details Effect', *Educational Psychology Review* 32(3): 707–734.

Sweller, J. (2012), 'Cognitive Load Theory' in Seel, N.M. (ed) *Encyclopedia of the Sciences of Learning.* Boston: Springer.

Sweller, J. and Chandler, P. (1994), 'Why some material is difficult to learn'. *Cognition and Instruction* 12:185–233.

Tiffany, S. (2023), *Mr T Does Primary History.* California: Corwin.

Tunzelmann, A. (2021) 'Why history deserves to be at the movies', *What is History, Now?* London: Weidenfeld and Nicolson

Van Kesteren, K.T.R. and Meeter, M. (2020), 'How to optimize knowledge construction in the brain,' *Science of learning* 5(1):5.

Weinstein, Y., Sumeracki, M. with Caviglioli, O. (2018), *Understanding How We Learn.* Abingdon: Routledge.

Wilkinson, A. (1965), 'The Concept of Oracy'. *Educational Review,* 17(4), 11–15.

Willingham, D.T. (2002), 'The Privileged Status of Story', *The American Federation of Teachers* https://www.aft.org/ae/summer2004/willingham.

Willingham, D.T. (2009), 'Why Don't Students Like School?' *American Educator* 33(1):4–13.

Wineburg, S. S. (1991), 'On the Reading of Historical Texts: Notes on the Breach between School and Academy'. *American Educational Research Journal,* 28(3): 495–519.

Wineburg, S. (1998), 'Reading Abraham Lincoln: An Expert/Expert Study in the Interpretation of Historical Texts'. *Cognitive Science,* 22: 319–346.

Witherby, A. E., and Carpenter, S. K. (2022), 'The rich-get-richer effect: Prior knowledge predicts new learning of domain-relevant information'. *Journal of Experimental Psychology: Learning, Memory, and Cognition.* 48(4): 483–498.

Woodcock, J (2005), 'Does the linguistic release the conceptual? Helping Year 10 to improve their casual reasoning'. *Teaching History,* 119: 5–14.

Wrenn, A. (2011), 'Significance' in Davies, I. (ed) *Debates in History Teaching.* Abingdon: Routledge, pp.148–158.

Young, M. and Lambert, D. (2014), *Knowledge and the Future School: Curriculum and Social Justice.* London: Bloomsbury.

Index